Pitt Series in

Policy and Institutional Studies

SCRAMBLING ▬ FOR ▬ PROTECTION

*The New Media and the
First Amendment*

PATRICK M. GARRY

University of Pittsburgh Press

Pittsburgh and London

For my father

Published by the University of Pittsburgh Press, Pittsburgh, Pa. 15260
Copyright © 1994, University of Pittsburgh Press
All rights reserved
Manufactured in the United States of America
Printed on acid-free paper

Library of Congress Cataloging-in-Publication Data

Garry, Patrick M.
    Scrambling for protection: the new media and the First Amendment /
Patrick M. Garry.
        p.   cm.
    Includes index.
    ISBN 0-8229-3798-0 (cloth : acid-free paper)
    1. Freedom of the press—United States.   2. Mass media—Law and
legislation—United States.   I. Title.
KF4774.G373   1994
342.73′0853—dc20   [347.302853]   94-14020
                                                              CIP

A CIP catalogue record for this book is available from the British Library.
Eurospan, London

CONTENTS

PART V
The Future of the First Amendment

PART I

The First Amendment at the Edge of Change

Changes in the nation's legal and constitutional fabric are difficult to predict. Yet, because of significant changes occurring in the media and in society's relationship with that media, the First Amendment press doctrines must also evolve to accommodate those developments. The changes involving the media will breed disputes that the courts will eventually have to decide, and those disputes will require the intervention of the First Amendment. The history of the American press and the First Amendment shows a correlation between changes in the former and those in the latter. At only three previous times, however, has the pattern of change come together to produce a significant transformation of First Amendment values. It appears that a fourth is about to occur.

1

Approaching Changes in First Amendment Press Doctrines

In 1991, the United States commemorated the bicentennial of the First Amendment, and journalists and media lawyers celebrated the press freedoms that had been won throughout the two-hundred-year history of the First Amendment. Yet while the nation reflected on its tradition of a free press, forces were already taking shape that would greatly change the direction of the First Amendment's third century.

It is somewhat unusual to speak of dramatic changes in First Amendment doctrines. The American constitution in many ways aims to inhibit or dampen change. While its pluralistic democracy provides an almost constant social flux, America's constitutional doctrines seek to control and minimize change. Because of this resistance, however, the pressures for constitutional change often build up to the point where a period of dramatic adjustment is unavoidable. Such is the case with the First Amendment press clause as it enters its third century.

The concept of imminent change seems somewhat inimical to the timeless and universal image of constitutional doctrines. According to the traditional legal model, judges and courts are supposed to be immune from the kind of social determinism that produces inevitable change. Yet constitutional law arises just like any other type of law—from conflicts and disputes within society. And as new areas of conflict arise, new constitutional doctrines must be forged to resolve those conflicts. Such conflicts are on the First Amendment horizon, and no matter how strong the resistance to constitutional change, these disputes will require new First Amendment press doctrines.

With the United States becoming ever more a media society, the First Amendment press clause will increasingly shape how society communicates. American society is in the midst of a "communications revolution." While the communications industries are undergoing rapid transformations, the government is making plans to build a national information infrastructure. Information itself has become the principal product of the national economy, and many business analysts predict that communications will be one of the strongest growth industries of the 1990s. The information and communications industries will occupy a larger place in the increasingly global economy as it challenges the traditional supremacy of the manufacturing and agriculture sectors. More newspapers, magazines, and television programs are produced in the United States than anywhere else in the world. In 1990, for instance, U.S. film and television producers earned more than $6.6 billion from foreign markets.[1]

In addition to its economy resting more heavily on communications and information, America's social identity is increasingly being shaped by the media. Television, for example, has become the common culture of those who have grown up with it; it contributes to their sense of being members of a nation.[2] While television used to be about big events such as presidential elections and moon walks, it is today a basic ingredient in daily life. Viewing talk shows replaces conversing with one's neighbor. Instead of talking about the day's events, a family on its evenings together may gather silently around the television set. Consequently, social and political leaders have looked to the media to provide the social cohesion once supplied by public spaces. Streets, squares, and parks have been largely displaced by telephones, television, and video recorders. Life in the media culture of modern America is increasingly experienced through the media, not just talked about in the media.

As American life more and more revolves around the media, the First Amendment press clause becomes an ever more important influence not only on press freedoms but on society itself. This relationship between American society and the First Amendment, however, is also a reciprocal one. While the First Amendment governs certain social relations with the media, changes in those relations in turn affect First Amendment doctrines. The amendment does not exist in a societal vacuum. Its evolution has been influenced by the evolution of American society, and its most dramatic periods of development have occurred when equally dramatic changes within society have produced the kind of disputes that required new First Amendment doctrines.

America is on the verge of a period of great change in its First Amendment press freedoms. There have been only three in the nation's history, with the last one only a couple of decades ago, but another period of dramatic change in the First Amendment is approaching and will focus primarily on the press clause, which states that "Congress shall make no law . . . abridging the freedom . . . of the press." This transformation will arise from significant changes taking place within the media and in the social and political role of the press.

With the introduction of new communications technologies, and with increased competition between the newspaper, broadcast, cable television, and telephone industries, the American press has entered a period of unprecedented metamorphosis. The traditional media, for instance, appears to be in a state of relative decline. Industry analysts argue that newspaper companies will never again reach the level of financial profitability that they reached in the 1980s or the readership numbers they achieved in the 1960s. Journalists likewise claim that an increasingly cost-conscious newspaper industry will never again devote the resources to news coverage that it once did. Furthermore, with an ever-hastening pace toward an all-electronic media system, the death of the ink-on-paper form of conveying information has been widely predicted.

In perhaps greater trouble than the newspapers are the television networks. In *Three Blind Mice,* Ken Auletta documents in detail the demise of the networks in the 1980s.[3] Given this decline in network power, many analysts predict that only two of the three major networks will survive into the twenty-first century. Moreover, as the financial health of the networks deteriorates, their news departments are being drastically reduced and scaled back. And with competition from Cable News Network (CNN) and other cable stations, the networks may further reduce or even eliminate their news divisions. This reduction reflects a more fundamental decline in network audience. With the explosion of cable television and video cassette recorders, fewer Americans are watching network television.

The rapid development of communication technologies is also forcing radical changes in the media field. Cable television in the future may provide hundreds of channels to each home. But cable may encounter stiff competition from the telephone companies, many of which are planning to challenge the newspaper industry by offering information services and vie for the television audience by sending video programming over their networks. Consequently, intense conflicts have arisen among the various media groups over the future regulation of the industry and the types of services to be provided by each group. Moreover, new kinds of communication services are emerging from direct broadcasting satellites and electronic information networks. Computer publishing, for instance, claims to be the press of the future.

The rapid evolution of technology has been matched by a flurry of economic and industry changes. Since 1992, merger and acquisitions activity in the communications industry has occurred at a dizzying pace. Bell Atlantic Corporation mounted an aggressive attempt to merge with Tele-Communications Inc. (TCI), the nation's largest cable provider. U.S. West, Inc. has invested in Time Warner. AT&T plunged back into the local telephone market with its acquisition of McCaw Cellular Communications Inc. And, in a Wall Street battle reminiscent of the 1980s, Viacom merged with Blockbuster. As government regulators have recognized, "the marketplace is changing under our feet completely, and we're going to have to do some quick-stepping to keep up with it."[4]

No matter what media entities survive and prosper in the next century, the media in general will change in its role toward the nonjournalist public. Technology is substantially expanding the number of people who can engage in communicative and press-related functions. No longer must the public assume a strictly passive or consuming role in the communication process. Interested persons will be able to better select the type of information they receive and to more effectively register their opinions and viewpoints. The future press will also be more oriented toward and customized to the individual and, through the use of interactive media, will be less focused on a mass audience. By allowing the public to participate directly in the selection of information and in the process of communication, the future press will lessen the public's dependency on the journalist and other intermediaries for its information and communication needs. In effect, the new media promises to involve a larger segment of the public in the information-sharing process.

In addition to changes in the economic and technological structure of the press, significant reforms may also be looming in the political role of the press. Popular dissatisfaction with the current state of ''media politics'' has brought increasing demands for a revision of the press' role in politics. The public's alienation from politics is believed to flow directly from its alienation from the press and from inadequate political information provided by the press. Critics complain that the media's obsession with superficial sound bites denigrates political dialogue. Social critic Christopher Lasch likewise contends that a connection exists between the shallowness of modern American journalism and the growing apathy of the American electorate. He argues that the news media have abandoned their historical role as forums for public debate and have become too willing to be conduits for information pumped out by publicists and other skilled media manipulators.[5] As monopolistic gatekeepers of information, the media is also attacked for excluding certain people and certain issues from the public dialogue.

With modern political campaigns relying increasingly on the media, pressure for political reform has translated into pressure to reform the press, to improve campaign coverage, and to elevate the quality of political dialogue. In fact, any future political reform seems to depend on changes in the role of the press in the political process. The more the media focuses its political dialogue on thirty-second sound bites, the fewer opportunities the public has to become involved in a search for long-term solutions to real social problems. Thus, demands for changes in the political role of the press focus largely on providing for a greater citizen involvement in the political dialogue through the press.

During recent presidential campaigns, voters have come to increasingly blame the news media for the perceived degeneration of presidential politics.[6] Given this mounting dissatisfaction with the press, it seems inevitable that the political role of the press will change, and the direction of this change will coincide with those fostered by the new media technologies—toward creating a press more responsive to and interactive with the public.

Both the technological advances and the social pressures for reform in the political role of the press will eventually lead to a new era in First Amendment press clause doctrines. The rapidly changing press will breed the kind of tensions and disputes that inevitably lead to constitutional resolution. With the newspaper, computer, telephone, broadcast, and cable industries fighting over who will control the future American press, and with each clamoring for different regulations and freedoms, the courts will ultimately be forced to settle these disputes. In doing so, they will have to define "the press," whose existence and activities deserve constitutional protection. Consequently, new First Amendment doctrines will emerge from the conflicts and tensions among the various media groups vying for legal protection and economic advantage.

A constitutional definition of the press is also needed to remedy the confusing and inconsistent regulatory scheme currently governing the media. Under the existing regulatory scheme, the print media receives different constitutional treatment than the broadcast media, which in turn is governed by principles distinct from the cable and telecommunications industries. A separate First Amendment standard applies to each technology. Such a scheme, however, will become nearly impossible to administer with the increasing diversity and numbers of new media technologies that will be available in the future.

In his landmark book *Technologies of Freedom,* the late Ithiel de Sola Pool proclaimed an optimistic belief about the future technological changes in the press and their effect on democratic society. To achieve such potential, however, the inconsistent and outmoded governmental regulations of the media would have to be eliminated, according to Pool.[7] Yet the demands of Pool and others to dismantle the current regulatory system have gone unfulfilled, perhaps because of the absence of any unified identity of the press that would in turn require a unified legal treatment. A constitutional definition of the press requiring consistent treatment for all types of press forums will be a necessary initial step in accomplishing such a reform of the American communications regulation.

In the past, the First Amendment press freedoms have been essentially tied to the existing media groups and institutions. The newspaper industry has certain freedoms, as do the broadcast, cable, and telephone industries. Overall, these freedoms have been created under a type of interest-group allocation process, but interest-group privileges and benefits—as demonstrated by the unpopularity of interest-group politics—have been subjected to a populist backlash by a public increasingly hostile to such freedoms.

In the future, however, a new definition of the press may give the First Amendment an applicability beyond specific media entities and groups of journalists. As the press expands its participation, more people will become involved in its information-sharing process. And as the First Amendment fans out its umbrella of protection to such a press, its freedoms will be exercised by the increasing number of people participating in that press. Consequently, the public may acquire a deeper stake in the First Amendment press clause.

During the last evolutionary stage of First Amendment press freedoms, the courts focused on the journalistic practices of newspaper and network television reporters. Such newsgathering activities, after all, were the subject of the disputes being litigated. Although judges never defined the constitutionally protected press, they more or less implicitly equated "the press" with professional journalists.

As new technologies and economic trends create a more interactive media less controlled by traditional journalists, however, the existing constitutional notions of "the press" may be inadequate to extend sufficient protection to this new media. For First Amendment doctrines to keep pace with a changing media in a changing society, the courts should define the press to include all the new technologies that facilitate social and political communication. Most particularly, the constitutional definition of the press should include the emerging interactive media that promises to provide a participatory communication forum for social and political dialogue, much like the role played by the eighteenth-century American press.

If current trends are indicative of the future, Americans increasingly will be getting more and more of their information from computer-based communications such as electronic bulletin boards, conferencing services, and computer networks. These communications systems obviously differ significantly from traditional media entities like newspapers and network television news divisions. Because of their accessibility to the general public, the new "computer-based forums for debate are witnessing perhaps the greatest exercise of First Amendment freedoms this country has ever seen."[8] If such technologies do indeed have the democratic potential that their supporters claim, it would be a grave mistake not to accord them constitutional protection, especially given the uphill battles they must wage against the powerful and entrenched traditional media corporations.

Only a functional approach to press freedoms—namely, protecting those press functions vital to the health of democratic society—will allow the First Amendment to accommodate all the technological and economic changes in the media. And only by recognizing the unique function that the new technologies are equipped to perform—the democratic dialogue function—can the courts adequately protect America's evolving press. This functional approach, specifically recognizing the emerging technologies that facilitate interactive communication, will take advantage of the rare opportunity presented by the changing media environment to reshape the future course of the First Amendment and of the press in a direction that serves the needs and values of a democratic society.

The impending evolutionary period in First Amendment press doctrines is predicted in part 1 of this book. This prediction is based on current developments in the media, as well as on historical experience. As argued in chapter 2, each previous evolutionary stage in First Amendment press doctrines was similarly accompanied by or preceded by transformations in the nation's media. The next evolutionary stage, however, will grapple with defining the constitutionally protected press in the information age of the twenty-first century.

Part 2 discusses the forces of change that will breed a new era in First Amendment press freedoms. Economic and technological changes in the existing media, along with the introduction of new communications technologies, will create disputes that will eventually come to the courts for resolution. In addition to these changes, demands for reforms in the political role of the press will further increase the pressure for change in both the media and First Amendment doctrines.

The necessity for transformation of current constitutional press doctrines will arise because the current ones cannot adequately accommodate the technological and political changes in the media. Part 3 analyzes the existing First Amendment model of the press—the fourth estate model—and its shortcomings in relation to the changing media. While the last stage of First Amendment evolution focused on protecting the journalistic press, the approaching one must concentrate on guarding a participatory press.

In forming a new model or definition of the press, it is helpful to examine the type of press that existed when the First Amendment was ratified, particularly since the eighteenth-century press has striking similarities to many of the new media technologies. Chapter 8 in part 4 looks back to the past in an attempt to define the constitutionally protected press of the twenty-first century. The remaining chapters in part 4 study the press clause and conclude that it protects only a press that performs certain social and political functions. By introducing a function not explicitly and formally recognized in previous First Amendment case law—that is, the democratic dialogue function—these chapters argue for the extension of constitutional protections to the new media.

The future application of the First Amendment in an age of technological and economic convergence in the media is discussed in part 5. This section argues that only a functional definition of the press can eliminate the contradictory and confusing regulatory environment currently governing the media. And only such a definition can support the positive potential of the new media.

2

Historical Patterns of Change in the First Amendment

ALTHOUGH INFREQUENT, periods of dramatic change in First Amendment press doctrines have previously occurred and were a result of significant changes in the press and in the ways in which society communicated. Media scholars have noted this historical relationship. A central theme of M. Ethan Katsh's *The Electronic Media and the Transformation of Law* is that changes in the means used to communicate information in turn bring changes in communications law, since that law has come to rely on the transmission of information in a particular way. According to Ithiel de Sola Pool, drastic changes in the press often translate into great changes in First Amendment practices.[1]

Every previous period of dramatic change in press clause doctrines has been preceded or accompanied by a corresponding change in the press. The ratification of the First Amendment was preceded by a greatly transformed eighteenth-century press. It developed out of a communications environment that had changed the flow of information dramatically and had done so in spite of numerous attempts to censor and control it (colonial censorship and licensing laws were formally repudiated by the First Amendment).[2] Preceding the break with England, a politically active and participatory press had developed in the colonies, revolutionary in its political activism and its independence from British colonial government. Nowhere in the world was the press so politically opinionated and democratic, and historians overwhelmingly agree that this newly developed political press greatly contributed to the movement for American independence.

The next period of change in First Amendment press doctrines occurred around the First World War.[3] During a time of social instability due to wartime fears, exploding immigration, urban crowding, and the threat of Bolshevik radicalism, the U.S. government prosecuted dissidents under a law forbidding criticism of the government's war efforts. These prosecutions were commonly aimed at immigrant radicals, socialists, and pacifists. During World War I and the years immediately following it, the right of expression was subjected to restrictions more widespread than at any previous time in American history.

The Espionage Act of 1917 imposed criminal penalties on any willful attempt to promote disloyalty in the armed forces or to obstruct recruitment. The Sedition Act of 1918 amended and broadened the Espionage Act by making it a crime to write or publish any disloyal, disrespectful, or abusive language about the United States government or its military. These laws also empowered the postmaster general to seize all newspapers, pamphlets, and circulars violating any provisions of the acts.

These acts were used to punish socialist, pacifist, and German-language newspapers.[4] The *American Socialist* was banned from the mails, as was *Solidarity,* the journal of the left-wing Industrial Workers of the World. A vociferous advocate of the Irish independence movement, Jeremiah O'Leary, lost mailing privileges for *Bull* because he opposed wartime cooperation with the British. And *The Masses* was banned for publishing an issue containing four antiwar cartoons and a poem defending certain radical leaders.

Altogether some forty-four papers lost their mailing privileges during the first year of the Espionage Act, and another thirty retained them only by agreeing to print nothing more concerning the war. The best known were two Socialist dailies, the *New York Call* and Victor Berger's *Milwaukee Leader.* For a time during and after the war, all incoming mail was prevented from reaching the *Leader,* and the Supreme Court upheld the post office ban on the *Leader* in a 1921 decision. The German-language press likewise was hit hard by mail bans and prosecutions, and its circulation during the war dropped to half of its prewar numbers.

Other papers that did not wholeheartedly support the government during this time also felt the force of public opposition. The

Hearst newspapers, which had bitterly opposed American entry into the war and had vigorously denounced the actions against the socialist and German-language newspapers, were widely attacked. Moreover, an issue of the *Nation* was held up in the New York post office because it carried an editorial titled "Civil Liberty Dead."

Beginning in the late nineteenth century and continuing through the 1920s, even the mainstream American press sought a wider and more popular audience, with the result that it soon became more democratic and representational of society. By the 1920s, newspaper readership exploded and the tabloid newspaper was born as the newspaper industry reached out to crowded and diverse urban populations. Both its content and its price appealed to the immigrant working class. In short, the diversity of the new American urban and immigrant population was finding expression in the press.[5]

This changing American press contributed to the first judicial statements on First Amendment doctrines and principles. During this evolutionary stage in the First Amendment, the Court focused on the question of whether individuals and the press were free to criticize the government and whether the country could tolerate dissent. For the first time, the Supreme Court heard cases involving First Amendment freedoms, but, in most of these cases, the Court ruled against the interests of free speech and press. Yet within this surge of First Amendment case law, several noteworthy decisions did hold in favor of First Amendment values. In *Masses Publishing Co. v. Patten,* 244 F. 535 (S.D.N.Y. 1917), the monthly revolutionary journal, *The Masses,* asked the court to prohibit the postmaster from denying it access to the mails under the Espionage Act of 1917. In the first pro–First Amendment decision in a federal court, Judge Learned Hand granted the publisher's request.

The Supreme Court, in its first judicial pronouncement on the First Amendment, upheld the constitutionality of the prosecutions under the Sedition and Espionage acts in *U.S. v. Schenck,* 249 U.S. 47 (1919). In response to *Schenck,* passionate opposition from respected legal scholars like Judge Learned Hand, Ernst Freund and Zechariah Chafee began to influence First Amendment thinking.[6] Inspired by this rush of First Amendment inquiry,

Oliver Wendell Holmes authored a vigorous dissent to future enforcement of the acts and offered an eloquent and moving defense of free speech and press in *Abrams v. U.S.,* 250 U.S. 616 (1919)—the first statement by a Supreme Court justice in support of the First Amendment and one which pointed the way to the next evolutionary stage of First Amendment press doctrines in the 1960s.[7]

The first time the United States Supreme Court ruled in favor of the First Amendment was in the landmark case of *Near v. Minnesota,* 283 U.S. 697 (1931). In *Near,* the state obtained an injunction forbidding a newspaper from publishing a series of articles charging that Minneapolis law enforcement officers were not aggressively investigating certain alleged gangsters. On appeal, however, the Supreme Court overturned the injunction as an unconstitutional prior restraint on the press.

The next major stage of evolution in First Amendment press freedoms occurred during the late 1960s and the 1970s in connection with such great upheavals in American society as Vietnam, the civil rights movement, and Watergate. As was the case during the late 1910s and 1920s, the evolutionary style occurred during a period of social tension and accompanied a period of great change in the press, in which investigative and adversarial journalism came to characterize the American media. Also transforming the press industry was the increasing professionalization of journalism. The proliferation of journalism schools, the growing recognition of journalism as a profession, and the increasing specialization of journalists significantly changed the practices and identity of the press.

During this period, cases involving the First Amendment poured into the courts. Most of the cases involved speech issues, but many specifically addressed the freedoms and powers of the press. These cases ultimately brought about significant changes in the First Amendment doctrines applicable to the press. One of the most famous cases, and indeed one of the first cases in this transformational period, created a substantially revised libel doctrine for the press. *New York Times Co. v. Sullivan,* 376 U.S. 254 (1964), involved a libel action brought by L. B. Sullivan, a commissioner of the city of Montgomery, Alabama, against the *New York Times* for having published a full-page advertisement entitled "Heed Their Rising Voices," which charged that local officials in the South had harassed, falsely arrested, assaulted, and intimidated civil rights leaders and activists. The trial court ruled against the *New York Times* and awarded Sullivan damages. The Supreme Court, however, overturned the verdict and in the course of its decision gave the press much greater freedoms from future liability in libel actions. According to the Court's new libel doctrine, a public figure suing for libel must prove that the press acted with actual malice or with reckless disregard for the truth in publishing its story. The *Sullivan* decision obviously gave greater freedom to the press to criticize the government and to publish unpopular ideas.

In another case, brought several years after *Sullivan,* the Court gave even greater freedom to the press to act as a watchdog on government. In *New York Times Co. v. United States,* attempted to obtain an injunction forbidding the *New York Times* to publish a top-secret Defense Department study of the Vietnam War. The newspaper had obtained the study, known as the Pentagon Papers, from Daniel Ellsberg, a former Pentagon official. The Court held that such an injunction violated the First Amendment as an impermissible prior restraint against the press.

In addition to insulating the press from the harsh hand of the government, the Court also shielded the press from the public. In *Miami Herald Publishing Co. v. Tornillo,* 418 U.S. 241 (1974), the Court struck down a Florida "right of reply" statute. The statute required that a newspaper that assailed the personal character of any candidate for political office must provide to that candidate free of financial charge an opportunity to reply to the newspaper's charges. In holding that the statute violated the editorial freedoms and functions of the newspaper, the Court in *Tornillo* further protected an adversarial press from a public unhappy with its reporting.

The Court continued to expand the First Amendment protections for the journalistic practices of the mass media. A year after *Tornillo,* in *Cox Broadcasting Corp. v. Cohn,* 420 U.S. 469 (1975), the Court reversed a trial court judgment finding a television station liable for invasion of privacy because it had published the name of a rape victim.

In later decisions, the Court also granted to the press more freedom to practice its investigative journalism and to report on sensitive and disturbing subjects. For instance, in *Nebraska Press Association v. Stuart,* 427 U.S. 539 (1976), the Court held as an unconstitutional prior restraint a Nebraska trial judge's order in a well-known murder trial that the press refrain from publishing any confession or admission made by the defendant. A similar ruling occurred in *Landmark Communications, Inc. v. Virginia,* 435 U.S. 829 (1978), in which a newspaper, after accurately reporting that a particular state judge was under investigation, had been convicted of violating a state statute prohibiting any person from divulging information about such investigations. The Court held the statute invalid, concluding that such information lies near the core of the First Amendment.

Several highly visible Supreme Court cases in the 1970s also involved the press' asserted right to gather news. These cases, in particular, reflected the adversarial and investigative nature of the new journalism. In *Branzburg v. Hayes,* 408 U.S. 665 (1972), the press claimed that subpoenas requiring journalists to testify about their news sources violated the freedom of the press. In *Pell v. Procunier,* 417 U.S. 817 (1974), *Saxbe v. Washington Post Co.,* 417 U.S. 843 (1974), and *Houchins v. KQED,* 438 U.S. 1 (1978), the press sought a right of access to government information that was not generally available to the public at large. Finally, recognizing a limited right of news gathering, the Court in *Richmond Newspapers v. Virginia,* 448 U.S. 555 (1980), held that the First Amendment guaranteed the right of the press to attend criminal trial proceedings. In his concurrence, Justice Stevens characterized the case as a watershed: "For the first time, the Court unequivocally holds that an arbitrary interference with access to important information is an abridgment of the freedom . . . of the press protected by the First Amendment" (p. 578). Consequently, *Richmond Newspapers* appeared like a Supreme Court endorsement of what journalists had long sought—a special privilege of access to government-controlled information.

The cases revolutionizing First Amendment press freedoms in the 1970s emanated from a transformed press, one that had radically changed in its role toward government and society. During Vietnam and Watergate, the press had become an adversary to government, a fourth estate striving to serve as a watchdog over the other branches of the American political system. Investigative reporting assumed greater importance to journalists, who were seeking to expose abuses of power. The adversarial role of the press also evolved from the growing sense of professional identity among journalists. Furthermore, the growing concentration of the press contributed to its image as an aggressive, independent institution safely insulated from the government and the rest of society.

As history has demonstrated, each of the three previous evolutionary stages of First Amendment press doctrines was accompanied by significant changes within the press itself. Likewise, the next period of change in press freedoms will arise from disputes involving the new communications technologies. The future challenges to First Amendment freedoms will concern incidents such as that involving the electronic newspaper *Phrack,* whose equipment was seized by the government and its editor prosecuted for allegedly publishing illegally obtained information about the 911 telephone system. This seizure occurred even though the Supreme Court ruled in 1971 that the *New York Times* could not be punished for publishing the Pentagon Papers during the height of the Vietnam War. Of course, *Phrack* is not yet the *New York Times;* it is an electronic newspaper that exists only on computer networks, and computer networks are like bulletin boards: any user can read them or "post" messages on them. All that is required to log on to such a computer bulletin board system is a personal computer, a phone line, and a modem. By confiscating *Phrack* computers and software, the government effectively shut it down in retaliation for something it had published—a classic case of press restraint, if *Phrack* is considered "the press." Moreover, since approximately 35,000 computer networks currently operate in the United States, the experience of *Phrack* has potentially widespread implications.

In a similar development, although one not yet involving the government, recent experiences of Prodigy Services Company illustrate the challenges ahead for defining a free press in the computer age. Prodigy, a computer information and network service, was accused by the Anti-Defamation League (ADL) of allowing anti-Semitic statements on its electronic bulletin boards. Prodigy has 114 bulletin boards that carry 200,000 messages weekly. Operators of these bulletin boards remove illegal messages, such as proposed drug deals, as well as flagrantly defamatory material. Other than that, free speech reigns on the bulletin boards, which are advertised as open forums. The ADL dispute, however, raised the issue of whether Prodigy's computer networks enjoy First Amendment protection or whether they might be freely censored or regulated by the government in the future. In another area of budding conflict, intensifying censorship battles have already been reported on the academic computer networks.[8]

In addition to computer networks and bulletin boards, the new telecommunications technologies have also been the subject of much dispute. Newspaper and cable industries continue to challenge FCC decisions that allow the telephone companies to offer information services and to transmit television programming over telephone lines. Other regulatory pressures are being exerted against the newly developed caller-identification system and various types of call- or line-blocking schemes. And further regulation of 900-number telephone services seems imminent with repeated attempts having already been made by Congress and the FCC. Yet the same technology and equipment used to transmit sexually oriented messages are also providing consumers with information on general and business news, stock exchange reports, and job information. During the 1992 campaign, for instance, such services were used by both the candidates and various media organizations for the purpose of political communication with voters.

None of these technologies nor the attempted restrictions on them have received much First Amendment attention; nor have they attracted much attention from traditional press advocates. In fact, as with the opposition to telephone information services, the established media has actually opposed some of the new communications technologies. Yet the public and the courts should be concerned with these new technologies, for the nation is on the verge of a media revolution that might otherwise be stunted by unconstitutional restrictions. If left free to evolve, the press in the twenty-first century promises to be one more accessible to the individual and more conducive to interactive communication. It may offer a wider public opportunities for communication that have not been possible since the nation's birth. But to do so, it must receive constitutional recognition. According to the Electronic Frontier Foundation, a nonprofit organization dedicated to "extending constitutional rights to the realm of [the new communications technologies]," the "newest frontier for First Amendment freedoms is the electronic frontier."[9]

The approaching change in First Amendment doctrines will focus on the identity and structure of the press as it enters the twenty-first century. Decisions will have to be made, for instance, on how much constitutional protection cable television should have and whether Congress can regulate access to cable channels. In the previous evolutionary stages of press freedoms in the twentieth century, the focus was on the activities of the established press. During the 1920s, an increasingly democratic and urban press sought to express the nontraditional and dissident views of various elements of the new American population. During the 1960s and 1970s, an adversarial "fourth estate" press sought the freedom to aggressively investigate the abuses of government and to act as a check on all social forms of authority. In that role, the media organizations needed immunity from the inevitable libel actions and also needed certain powers to conduct their investigations against a secretive government. Throughout these struggles, the First Amendment underwent great change in the freedoms it granted to the *activities* of the press.

The constitutional focus in the future will increasingly be on *how* society communicates. Previous evolutionary stages of the First Amendment never focused on defining the nature of the press entitled to those protections. In the past, there was little need to define the press, since there was little conflict over the identity of that press. For instance, in the 1920s, the press comprised the circulating newspapers; in the 1970s, it still comprised the newspapers, with the addition of the broadcast news departments. Throughout the twentieth century, the press has been almost exclusively journalist-centered. All that, however, may be about to change.

Because the future changes in First Amendment doctrines will focus primarily on press identity and on the particular communications services that qualify for constitutional protection, the government will play a vastly different role in forging new First

Amendment doctrines. Contrary to the antagonistic view of the government it held several decades ago, the media now looks to the government as a partner and an ally. The newspaper, cable, broadcast, and telephone industries have each sought to enlist the assistance of government in structuring a media industry to their respective preferences. Media advocates, contrary to their counterparts of several decades ago, readily admit that the future of the communications media in the United States will be largely shaped by government policy. Thus, the approaching transformation of the First Amendment will be characterized by shifting roles and relationships between the press and the government. Because of this changing relationship, the need to constitutionally define the press becomes all the more urgent. For without defining the type of press that is immune from government restriction, the danger of unconstitutional regulation increases.

In the past, lawyers and their traditional media clients have shaped the First Amendment on a case-by-case basis without defining the constitutionally protected press. The changing media and the fundamental shift in the nature of future litigation disputes, however, give courts the opportunity to redefine and reexamine the values and purposes of the type of press protected by the First Amendment.

■ PART II ■

Agents of Change

An approaching period of significant change in First Amendment press doctrines will follow a period of equally significant change in the American press. Such transformations in the press have already begun and will continue to intensify. Technological and economic developments, along with demands for modifying the political role of the press, will dramatically transform the existing press over the coming decade. This change will inevitably lead to new First Amendment doctrines relating to the identity and nature of the constitutionally protected press.

The changing press by itself might not necessarily prompt a rewriting of First Amendment doctrines; however, changes in the media are breeding disputes that will ultimately arrive in the courts. And it is there that press doctrines will have to be reexamined and reformulated.

3

The Changing Press

IMPENDING CHANGE often causes immediate insecurity and inner turmoil. A family facing the prospect of moving to a new city or having a parent laid off from employment will usually initially respond with increased family quarrels and conflicts. In a corporation about to be acquired by another, the first reaction among employees is a struggle for a position of survival. Likewise, the first sign that the American media is about to radically change can be seen in the explosion of intramedia conflicts. As with most other industries or organizations, current media groups are busy trying to resist or influence the impending changes by building or breaking down certain regulatory barriers to those changes.

The approaching period of metamorphosis in the media is perhaps best reflected by the current "media wars" being fought among the newspaper, telephone, cable, and broadcast television industries. These industry groups are battling one another for control of various aspects of the country's future communications system. The battle is being fought in Congress and at the Federal Communications Commission (FCC), and it is the result of regulatory and technological developments that now make each industry a potential competitor in the information marketplace.

The intramedia conflicts precede inevitable competition in the marketplace; yet, before this competition can take place, intricate and outdated regulatory barriers must be removed. Consequently, the initial phases of the current media wars are being waged at the governmental rather than the economic level.

25

The FCC provides the site of most of the media battles. Under Chairman Alfred Sikes, the FCC encouraged more competition in the media marketplace. Indeed, Sikes pushed the FCC into developing a national communications system and breaking down the barriers that insulate various media industries from competition. His vision of America's media future included a television set that would receive four hundred channels and contain a home computer, a telephone, and a library capable of storing the contents of every book ever written. It would be interactive, meaning a viewer can take educational courses or participate in a city council meeting without ever leaving the house.[1] Such a vision, however, involves the convergence and interaction of many presently separated communications technologies.

As technologies have both proliferated and converged, the FCC now oversees a massive and growing collection of telecommunications businesses. Consequently, it has become the traffic cop in a communications revolution. The decisions it makes in the near future will be critical in shaping who controls the nation's electronic information channels, how that information is delivered, and even how the electorate communicates and receives information about the issues of the day. Some of the issues facing the FCC include:

1. setting a national standard for high-definition television;
2. reallocating frequencies on the broadcast spectrum, the invisible band of electromagnetic waves used by television and radio stations, cellular phone companies, and pocket pagers;
3. relaxing restrictions that limit the number and kind of media properties a company may own. (Current FCC rules prevent a single company from owning more than twelve AM radio stations, twelve FM stations, and twelve local television stations, or more than one of each type of property in a single market);
4. overhauling regulations that would streamline the way the FCC licenses and regulates radio operators;
5. reforming the cable television industry by bringing more competition into that industry; and

6. opening local phone service to competition by requiring existing local monopolies to make their lines available to competitors.

Under Chairman Sikes, the FCC also proposed a radical idea—allowing the telephone companies to become carriers of television programming. Under this proposal, the phone companies would string fiber-optic wires carrying hundreds of programs into homes. Fiber-optic lines are capable of carrying not only computer information but also hundreds of electronic services and video images as well. As such, they have the potential to replace over-the-air broadcasting, cable television, and even the familiar telephone line.

This "video dial tone" approach obviously raises the hire of the newspaper and cable industries, which want to keep a major new competitor out of its business, but it also involves another serious concern of the phone companies, which claim the need to be in the programming business to justify the cost of laying fiber-optic lines—a task which may cost as much as $200 billion. Taken as a whole, Sikes's agenda has raised important questions in the minds of those in the media and communications businesses. If the walls currently keeping media and telecommunications businesses apart do come down, which of the four "data highways" that now enter the home—cable television, broadcast television and radio signals, phone wires, and satellite transmissions—will survive into the twenty-first century?

The controversy in the FCC over the future structure of the nation's communications industry stems in part from the July 1991 ruling by U.S. District Judge Harold Greene in *U.S. v. Western Electric Co.,* 767 F. Supp. 308 (D.D.C. 1991), which opened the door to the seven regional Bell operating companies ("telcos") to offer information services, video on demand, electronic messaging, and mail and transaction services such as home shopping. Judge Greene's ruling laid the foundation for dismantling old regulatory schemes and building more competition. In response to this ruling, and fearful of the uncertainty of future competition, newspaper publishers, broadcasters, cable operators, and other information service providers began pressing for legislation that would impose additional conditions on the entry of the telephone companies into this business.

Because of Judge Greene's ruling, the telcos are finally in a position to enter the information age—and indeed to create it, since they will also have to provide the infrastructure to deliver the information services. The telephone companies had previously been excluded from this business because they controlled the conduit by which the information reaches the subscriber—the telephone network. And the fear is that, if allowed to enter the business, the telephone companies will use this control to freeze out all other competitors from the telephone networks. This fear of telephone monopoly, however, had been the motivation behind the initial ban on telephone companies offering their own information services, which was overruled by Judge Greene.

Shortly after Judge Greene lifted the judicial restrictions preventing the telephone companies from entering the information services business, the telcos received yet another boost. On 24 October 1991, the FCC proposed that local telephone companies be allowed to package and transmit television programming over local phone lines and that long-distance telephone companies be permitted to buy cable television systems. Such rules would expose cable companies to their most threatening competition yet. Indeed, the commission recommended that telephone companies be allowed to offer a "video dial tone" over telephone lines capable of carrying television programming. Initially, telephone companies would serve primarily as pipelines, not as program producers. But the FCC said phone companies should eventually be allowed to package and perhaps produce video programming, as long as they make their networks available to all programmers.

The video dial tone proposal thus marked the second major change in longstanding restrictions on the telephone companies' abilities to move into new information and programming services. The first effect of this has been to threaten the existing media with substantially increased competition. As an FCC spokesperson explained, "Both program providers and consumers would have choices they don't have today, without the bottlenecks provided by cable companies and without the bottlenecks of broadcasting."[2]

With deregulation and technological innovation, nearly every facet of the American media has been opened up to competition from the telephone companies. Industries that had previously been insulated by regulatory and technological walls are now having to compete in the battle for the new communications system of the future. Telephone companies, publishers, and cable and broadcast television firms are all fighting for turf.

The first rule of increased competition is that the current players oppose it; with the survival of entire industries and the revenues of billions of dollars at stake, they fight intensely. Such has been the case with the emerging media wars. Competition has translated into conflict, and these conflicts involve practically every actor in the entire U.S. communications field. Though competition and conflict potentially exists at every level of the communications system, the primary controversies have arisen among the major media groups: newspaper, broadcast and cable television, and telephone. Each separate industry is pursuing a different agenda and seeking different regulatory schemes.

The threat of the phone companies providing news, advertising, and television programs over the same wires that supply 95 percent of U.S. homes with basic phone service particularly frightens the newspaper industry. Newspapers are also facing the threat of competition from telephone companies wanting to create and transmit electronic newspapers. In February 1992, for instance, Congress began hearings into whether the Bell telephone companies should be allowed to gather and disseminate news and advertising in direct competition with newspapers.

The phone company's reach into the newspapers' territory could not have come at a worse time; newspaper publishers are stuck in the worst advertising slump in thirty years. Classified-advertising revenue, the lifeblood of newspapers, dropped more than 8 percent from 1991 to 1992, and only 62 percent of adults read newspapers, down from 78 percent twenty years ago. Furthermore, newspapers must buy network time from phone companies if they want to publish and transmit electronic publications. In some regions, newspapers contend that phone companies have delayed providing phone lines for competing information services while launching services of their own. Though newspapers are already creating electronic newspapers and sending them to home computer terminals over the phone lines, publishers also claim that the telephone company does not provide such lines on a timely basis.[3] Some publishers fear that teaming with the phone company may be inevitable: "Today, the phone companies are just the provider of lines, but in the future, who knows?" said Michael Pulitzer, president of Pulitzer Publishing Company, publisher of the *St. Louis Post-Dispatch;* "It's hard to argue with technology."[4]

The telephone is increasingly becoming a delivery system for the more traditional press. For instance, according to the American Newspaper Publishers Association, 150 newspapers now provide free interactive voice services; more than five hundred offer 900 numbers or other pay-telephone services for access to a variety of full-text data bases; eleven offer a fax delivery of the next day's headlines; and seven offer local consumer-oriented videotex services using home computers or terminals.[5] New York's *Newsday,* for instance, has reported that it has formed a partnership with NYNEX to deliver local news by telephone.

In response to this threat from the telcos, the newspaper industry has turned to the government in an effort to preserve its position in the media marketplace and to insulate itself from the changing technological environment. It has geared up for a big legislative fight with the telephone companies. The industry supports a bill introduced by U.S. Representative Jim Cooper that is designed to put a roadblock in the path of the telephone companies' expansionist ideas. Cooper's proposed legislation would preclude a phone company from providing electronic publishing and information services within its region unless similar services are available from a competing phone network. The Cooper bill prohibits the Bell Telephone companies from entering the information services business until the FCC determines that at least 50 percent of all businesses and residences in the area have ready access to comparable telephone services and that at least 10 percent of those businesses and residences are customers of the phone companies' potential competitors. Because the majority of households are served by one local phone company, however, the bill would effectively lock phone firms out of new businesses.

If the telcos are allowed to enter the electronic publishing market, they would be able to produce electronic yellow pages that would cut into the newspaper industry's primary source of revenue—classified advertising. The American Newspaper Publishers Association (ANPA) has argued that without appropriate safeguards the telcos could exploit their monopoly control of indispensable facilities—the local telephone switches and wires—to stifle competition and eliminate diversity in the information services marketplace.

In this vein, ANPA has attacked the telephone companies for their history of anticompetitive behavior and has cited a litany of instances when they have abused their monopoly position in local telephone service and were fined for doing so. It argues that unless Congress acts, future "infotechnology" would be commandeered by the nation's most accomplished monopolists. This argument intensified when the Consumer Federation of America charged that the regional Bell companies have overcharged consumers by thirty billion dollars since 1984. Raising fears of an abusive telephone monopoly over information, the group likewise urged Congress to pass the Cooper bill.[6]

A minority of newspaper executives, however, believe the battle with the Bell companies is one the industry should not wage. Al Neuharth, former chairman of Gannett, argues that "publishers—the same conservative element that was pretty damn sure TV would not survive, some of whom are not convinced radio is here to stay—should seek to cooperate rather than fight with the Bells to get these new services on-line." "What you have is the champions of the free press saying 'Stop free enterprise,' " Neuharth says, echoing one of the phone company's central arguments. He further argues that "The First Amendment doesn't belong to newspaper publishers, or to the Baby Bells for that matter. It belongs to the people. They deserve the right to get their news when they want it, where they want it and how they want it."[7] Neuharth also labeled as sheer folly the request to Congress to act on the controversy: "It flies in the face of those First Amendment words, 'Congress shall make no law.' "

The battle between newspapers and the telephone companies, according to industry and congressional officials, "is likely to shape the nation's telecommunications future as no other event since the 1984 breakup of the telephone system." The lobbying war between the newspaper and telephone industries has been called "one of the most expensive lobbying battles in all congressional history."[8] Of course, the focus of the battle is monopoly power. The newspapers are called monopolies by the telephone companies, which claim that the industry is in desperate need of competition. But the newspapers argue that once the Bell Telephone companies enter the information field, they'll have a stranglehold on competitors, since they supply phone service to as much as 99 percent of the homes and businesses in their areas.

Perhaps more so than the newspaper industry, the cable industry is acutely concerned about competition from the telephone companies. Though newspapers have become monopolies through economic evolution, cable television from the beginning was a created monopoly, resulting not from natural economic forces but from burdensome regulations imposed by city governments themselves.

The FCC's recent ruling on video dial tone is something the regional phone companies have awaited for years—an early step in removing the barriers that prevent them from delivering television. If the telcos get their way, they will be able to compete directly with the cable television industry, giving consumers in previously monopolized markets a real choice for the first time.

The cable industry promotes a far different vision of the future. It describes the advantages of a "multiwire" world in which direct-broadcast television satellites, cellular phones, multimedia computer software, and cable television coexist. Such a vision, according to cable advocates, is the future the phone companies fear most—booming competition. Yet this same argument is also used by the phone companies against the cable industry—right now, according to the telcos, the cable industry is not subject to any effective competition.

Increasing competition, however, looms on the cable horizon. Competition will most likely increase within the cable industry, as analysts predict that each home may be able to receive up to four hundred different channels. Intensifying this competitive environment will be the independent programmers and the motion picture studios who will supply programming, as well as the telephone companies if they are ultimately permitted to furnish television programming. The cable industry may also face intense competition from direct broadcasting satellite systems. The race to control tomorrow's television and telecommunications businesses has set off a classic political battle in Washington. To fight the battle, the cable industry has been building political alliances with some of its most bitter enemies—broadcasters, consumer groups, and newspaper publishers. Broadcasters fear the phone companies as another competitor for television advertising dollars and audiences; newspaper publishers fear the phone industry will offer video newspapers and sophisticated electronic classified ads over a fiber-optic network. Consumer groups, who have attacked cable operators in the past as price gougers, have also reluctantly cast their lot with the cable industry by opposing relaxation of the current restrictions on the phone industry.

While the debate rages, cable companies are touting their own experiments with fiber optics. By adding signal-squeezing digital compression technology and installing fiber-optic lines in the main trunks of a cable system, thereby avoiding the huge expense of wiring every home, cable systems in a few years could be outfitted to offer as many as four- or five-hundred channels of service. Several cable companies are also responding to the phone industry's encroachment with a reciprocal strategy: to compete with the telcos on their own turf by attempting to start local phone service through so-called personal communications networks (PCNs). Like cellular phone networks, PCNs transmit conversations through radio transmission. The PCN phones would also be cheaper and have a clearer sound than existing cellular phone systems. And the PCN services could include pocket telephones and paging systems that allow a person to be "followed" anywhere by his or her phone number and facsimile machines and hand-held computers that communicate over the air. Some telecommunications experts even think that these wireless networks could eventually replace many conventional telephones.

The nation's biggest cable companies have invested hundreds of millions of dollars in an aggressive bid to compete against the local telephone industry. As of early 1992, thirty cable companies had obtained federal licenses to build experimental wireless telephone networks. On a different level, some large cable companies purchased businesses that were in competition with the local telephone companies to provide high-speed communications to big corporate customers. Through this expansion and diversification, according to George Gilder, "the cable TV industry is changing from being a video entertainment source to being a full-service telecommunications supplier." For instance, through a service called X*press offered by Tele-Communications Inc., the country's largest cable operator, subscribers can plug their personal computers into their cable television system's coaxial cable outlet and receive a huge flow of digitalized data. Ultimately, some experts believe X*press will be able to keep pace with centralized on-line data base services like Dow Jones or Dialog.[9]

To become full-fledged phone-service providers, however, the cable industry will need Congress to repeal restrictions that keep cable companies out of that business. Consequently, the tensions of competition continue to cause conflicts in the regulatory arena—conflicts which may inevitably end up in the courts and involve First Amendment press doctrines. The 1992 Cable Act, for instance, faced "a blizzard of lawsuits" from the cable industry.[10]

While the telcos and the cable industry combat each other, the broadcast television industry has opposed them both. Indeed, the current media wars come at a difficult time for broadcast television. In a June 1991 report, the FCC noted that "broadcast television has suffered an irreversible long-term decline in audience and revenue share, which will continue throughout the current decade." It concluded that "television broadcasting will be a smaller and far less profitable business in the year 2000 than it is now." Unless the long-term trend of revenue decline reverses, according to the report, "a shakeout could well occur."[11]

This bleak picture has prompted broadcasters to take their case both to the FCC and to Capitol Hill, arguing that laws and regulations have skewed the media marketplace in favor of their competitors. To achieve "equity," they want nothing less than the imposition of a sweeping set of regulations on cable operators. Denying that they simply want the government's help in retrieving their once-dominant role in television, broadcasters insist they only want a marketplace unencumbered by outdated regulations that make them less competitive. The Financial Interest and Syndication rules, which bar the networks from the lucrative syndication market, represent one such regulation.

Another segment of the broadcast industry, consisting principally of the local independent stations that are unaffiliated with a network, has a different legislative priority. These local stations want to require cable systems to carry their signals. In support of this claim, they cite a recent report of the Senate Commerce, Science, and Transportation Committee that found that "noncarriage" of local over-the-air broadcasting systems "is a serious problem" that threatens diversity of choice for viewers.[12]

In seeking stiffer cable regulations, broadcasters frame their arguments not just in terms of economic competition but in terms of their unique contribution to American life. According to Laurence Tisch, CBS Inc.'s chairman and chief executive officer, at stake in this conflict "is the future viability of our traditional system of universal free television." He expresses concern that unfair cable competition jeopardizes the role of free television as a "unifying force" in bringing the country together, as it did through the coverage of the Kennedy assassination and the Persian Gulf War. The result would be the atomizing of American culture and the dispersion of viewership into thousands of different choices.[13]

To many social observers, the erosion of the networks' power and influence has raised fears of social fragmentation. Whatever its failings, a mass medium like network television has been said to create a sense of community, and the television networks, by constituting a common communications system, have often brought a disparate population together to share an experience. Such a role was fulfilled when the networks became the nation's common gathering place after Martin Luther King, Jr., was assassinated or when the first moon landing occurred. Though during their prime the networks were criticized for imposing conformity upon an otherwise diverse American society, they now often provide the only common link among the citizens of a pluralistic and expansive nation. Though the networks were once criticized as elitist and repressive monopoly powers, one might now see them as a democratizing force, insofar as they offer free television to all citizens regardless of income, race, or educational background.

This change of attitude toward the networks, and the corresponding anxiety about the future of American community, is a result of sympathy for the networks' reversals of fortune. Indeed, the once-impenetrable strength of the three national networks was severely strained in the 1980s, and many in television feared this medium might itself follow radio's course when centralized command of national networks fell prey to localism and to a fragmentation that ended radio's reign as a medium with a national voice. Many critics fear that increasing competition from the cable and telephone industries will further erode the network's influence and increasingly contribute to a fragmented American society.[14] Due to new "narrowcasting" capabilities of cable, for instance, the specialized audience may replace the general audience, and a unified society may give way to a fragmented one.

The cable industry, however, dismisses these fears and argues that broadcasters are simply looking for a government bailout to escape the consequences of poor business judgments. Indeed, according to Henry Geller, a former general counsel of the FCC, "in the long run, over-the-air broadcasting may very well be doomed . . . and what's wrong with that? Nothing is forever. . . . People thought radio would be dominant forever, and along came television and reduced radio to something entirely different."[15]

Yet the broadcasters' attacks on the cable industry have had some success. In the face of growing consumer unrest, Congress enacted the 1992 Cable Act, which imposed new regulations on cable. The battle between broadcast and cable television also has shifted into the area of broadcast ownership regulations, which former FCC chairman Alfred Sikes recommended liberalizing various broadcast ownership restrictions that limit the total number of stations a company may own as well as the number allowed within a single market. Broadcasters claim these restrictions prevent them from achieving certain economies of scale that would strengthen their competitiveness. As Sikes explained, "The nature of the business here at the FCC is that we have a lot of old rules and a lot of new realities."[16] A still more important issue about cross-ownership is whether the owner of a physical cable may be the programmer of the system or must be only a common carrier.

The broadcast radio industry is also embroiled in the media wars at the FCC and faces numerous challenges because industry revenues are depressed, and new technologies, such as Digital Audio Broadcasting (DAB), are changing traditional structures. DAB plans to digitize radio broadcast signals and provide clearer sound, which may also stimulate a reorganization of the industry on many levels. First, the industry must decide key issues in such areas as copyright and AM-FM band parity. In addition, such competing technologies as digital satellite broadcasting and digital cable radio are under development. Both alternatives may directly compete for the broadcast radio audience.

In Congress and at the FCC, these pressures on the radio industry are translating into new regulations. In January 1992, for instance, the FCC approved a two-way radio service that gives consumers access to data services over their television sets. Under the basic technology approved by the FCC, consumers would essentially use mini-transmitters plugged into their televisions to send and receive signals, allowing them to shop electronically, respond to polls, and interact with other services. Moreover, in a recently released staff report, the FCC concluded that radio stations are in tight competition for limited advertising revenue, and that the industry is ailing. To assist the radio industry, enduring its worst recession in decades, the FCC subsequently loosened its restrictions on radio station ownership. In its revised rules, the commission more than doubled the number of radio stations that a single company could own and also allowed a single owner to have as many as three AM and three FM stations in a single city. According to the FCC, the old rules had long been outdated because radio stations face ample competition from cable television and other forms of communication. This same desire to liberalize ownership rules is influencing efforts aimed at eliminating a regulation that currently prohibits the three television networks from owning cable television systems.[17]

These media wars reflect a press that is undergoing substantial change. The focus of that change is on the structure of the press and media industry—an industry entering an era of dramatically increased competition. Indeed, perhaps the single greatest element of change affecting the press is increasing competition. Though such competition causes great uncertainty over the future makeup of the press, and though it causes dislocating tensions, it must also be remembered that absence of competition was the most criticized aspect of the press during the last couple of decades. The rising competition among the Bell telephone companies, for instance, reflects the changing trend of competitiveness. They are aggressively battling each other to establish a foothold in the new markets now open to them—video programming and information services. Although Southwestern Bell was the first to move into cable television, U.S. West and Bell Atlantic soon followed with their investments in Time Warner and Tele-Communications Inc. Moreover, with its purchase of McCaw Cellular, AT&T became a direct competitor of the Bell telephone companies in the wireless market. None of this cutthroat competition, however, was predicted back on January 1, 1984, when AT&T officially spun off the Baby Bells into separately owned local telephone companies. The 1993 acquisition by U.S. West of a 25 percent interest in Time Warner's entertainment division, for instance, was said to be "certain to ignite competition over local phone service, turning on its ear the conventional wisdom that the telephone and cable industries were on a collision course."[18]

Now that such competition has arrived, society should greet it with at least some degree of optimism. As has already been discussed, the television networks are facing more competition from cable television; in the future, they could experience even more competition from television programming offered over the telephone lines. After its performance during the Gulf War, for instance, CNN has proved to be a formidable challenger to network news. Yet in addition to this increased competition from outside the networks, the success of the Fox network has injected more competition within the network television industry itself. Not since the DuMont Television Network went out of business in 1955 have there been four networks in America.

Cable has also begun to compete with newspapers. Traditionally, local news coverage has been the almost-exclusive province of daily and weekly newspapers. They have provided the primary coverage of grass-roots news like city council elections, zoning board disputes and high school football. In the near future, however, twenty-four hour cable news operations may challenge the newspapers' hold on local news. In 1992, for instance, Time Warner began its twenty-four-hour cable news operation in New York City and will consequently have more news time to fill in one day than a network news division gets in weeks. C-Span will also increasingly compete with newspapers as it sponsors in the future round-the-clock press conferences, call-ins, debates, hearings, and key speeches.[19] Finally, specialized cable channels like Court TV promise to provide expertise and coverage not available in general-interest newspapers and television news programs.

Because of the increasing competition in the media, it is also unclear which media technologies will eventually emerge—high-definition television, direct-broadcast satellites, fiber optics, digitized signals, among countless others. Currently, the video communications business is dominated by five major powers—the networks, cable, the independent and affiliated stations, the Hollywood studios, and the telephone companies. Each is competing for control of the new technologies, and this competition is made more uncertain by the future regulatory stance of the federal government.

No one can know which of the major media powers will join forces to shape a vertically integrated communications system of the future and which industry will lapse into slow decline.[20] The telephone companies could become the distribution arm for Hollywood or the network programmers. The networks could become a cooperative, with affiliates cementing a partnership through common ownership. Direct-broadcast satellites could make all distributors, from stations to networks to cable companies, obsolete. And free television could become extinct.

Although increased competition will undoubtedly intensify conflicts and disputes within the media, it may already be improving the press in various subtle ways. For instance, in response to the threat of rising competition, the print media is seeking to better respond to the needs and interests of its audience. In its "News 2000" program, the Gannett Company is trying to remold the newsroom and beat structures of its newspapers to respond to perceived reader interests. This program also seeks to encourage Gannett's local newspapers to pay greater attention to community issues. Indeed, there seems to be a greater awareness that newspapers must embrace the concept of sharing the creation of the news: "There needs to be a willingness and openness to let the readers have a much greater hand in determining what's the news," says Richard Baker, director of corporate communication for CompuServe, a computer communications company with more than 900,000 subscribers.[21]

General-interest national magazines like *Time, Newsweek,* and *U.S. News & World Report,* for instance, are offering selective binding services that allow advertisers to place their ads in only those magazines going to certain targeted subscribers. *Newsweek* also offers its subscribers customized editions tailored to their particular interests. A subscriber, for instance, can have a nonfiction book excerpt bound into the magazine once a month, or have eight pages of expanded international coverage, or receive an additional section on money management or science. "The possibilities for selective binding have increased exponentially with the pressure to bond with readers," said James R. Guthrie, executive vice president for marketing of the Magazine Publishers of America. This effort also marks the first time that a customized section of a magazine will be paid for by subscribers instead of by advertisers, since *Newsweek*'s customized editorial sections will contain no advertising. In another significant change for the general-interest magazine industry, *Time* announced in 1993 that it would provide an electronic forum in which readers can hold two-way discussions on their computer terminals with the magazine's reporters and editors.

Because of increased competition, the newspaper industry will also continue to change, perhaps even dramatically, over the coming decades because advertising will no longer be able to provide two-thirds of the revenue stream. But perhaps that diminishing of advertising influence will in fact have a positive influence: newspapers have been more competitive and of higher quality when readers have paid a bigger share of newspaper revenues.[22]

Yet this additional competition for advertisers does not automatically portend doom for the newspapers, which have been in the advertising business longer than any other medium. Indeed, history shows that the instant communications of radio changed newspapers, that television changed radio and newspapers, and that cable is causing television to change—but that all forms of media survived. Eventually print will change because it will be easier to deliver the latest edition over fiber-optic phone lines to a facsimile machine in the customer's house. The newspaper will be tailored to the household's special interests (with an extra section on law for lawyers, for instance). Advertising may appear mostly in special sections aimed at special interest groups and be less than 50 percent of a newspaper's revenue base. And in a way, newspapers of the future will have returned to the newspaper model of the past, insofar as they are more responsive to and financially supported by the reader. Some newspapers, like the *Minneapolis Star Tribune* and the *Charlotte Observer,* are already seeking to involve their readers in the news-coverage process to a greater extent. These newspapers, acting on the presumption that the more their readers participate in the newspaper the more they will support it, have organized reader panels to comment on news coverage, provided interactive information services, and sponsored reader discussion groups on issues of local concern.

Although the potentially increasing competition may improve the existing media, it will also produce intense media battles and conflicts which will inevitably play out in governmental and judicial arenas. Shortly after it announced its merger plans with Tele-Communications Inc., for instance, Bell Atlantic filed a lawsuit seeking to invalidate rules blocking telephone companies from owning cable television programming. The various participants in the battles that seek to define the new media environment have already sought to enlist the government as a beneficent partner. In the wake of AT&T's acquisition of McCaw Cellular, for instance, the Bell telephone companies petitioned the FCC to permit them to enter the long-distance market. The media is not looking at the government as an oppressor or as a censor, as it had in the past, but as a valuable partner capable of structuring a media industry turned upside down by regulatory, economic, and technological changes. This government involvement, however, will ultimately lead to resolution of many of the disputes in the courts.

With the major press battles occurring over the future structure and makeup of the media, the approaching changes in First Amendment doctrines will focus on defining the constitutionally protected ''press.'' With the Congress and FCC embroiled in disputes over the structure of the press, cases will soon come to the courts involving their legislative and regulatory decisions. The courts will then, in settling the First Amendment issues, have to define ''the press.''

The need to define ''the press'' will be heightened not only by the changing press but also by the convergence of media technologies. As most media analysts predict, the future will bring a natural convergence of all forms of media—the coming together of all communication technologies and functions into a single system, an integration of traditional print and electronic media. In the past, a broad moat separated the print media from the electronic ones. These two technologies did things differently enough to limit competition between them, though to a degree they competed in news, fiction, and pictures. Today, however, the technologies that underlie print, telephone, cable, and broadcast television are converging. The competition and convergence of electronic media with print, for instance, began with telegraphy, continued with broadcasting, and today is most striking with data or computer networks.[23]

In the coming era, the print and telecommunications media will no longer be kept apart by a fundamental difference in their technologies. No longer can we view the media as separate technological functions like ink on paper and over-the-air broadcasting. Each media form will be intermingled with another; newspapers will be delivered electronically or over telephone lines. Technology will therefore unite and intermix the formerly separate media forms, and the economic and regulatory problems of the electronic media, for example, will also become the problems of the print media.[24]

This convergence is also reflected by the merger activity in the communications field. The 1993 Bell Atlantic–TCI merger, for instance, contradicted the conventional wisdom that telephone and cable companies would always be separate and antagonistic competitors in the media marketplace. Instead, the merger set in motion a drastic transformation of the nation's telecommunications structure, replacing regulated cable and local telephone monopolies with vigorously competing companies offering various information services. It has hastened the arrival of what Vice-President Gore has called "the information superhighway." Overall, the merger was described as "the total redefinition of the communications industry."[25]

The convergence of all types of communication into a single, electronically based, computer-driven mode will, in turn, allow the existing media forms to concentrate on their particular strengths and specialties. For instance, while the newspaper's role as information provider is under assault by electronic media and data bases, it does have two services that electronic data bases do not: well-edited, coherent news reports and, even more vital, opinions in editorial columns and op-ed pages. Opinion has always been a print media specialty. Although newspapers do not actively promote their opinion sections, such pages may be their most important and distinguishable asset. Thus, in the midst of the upcoming electronic transformation of the media, the key to the newspaper's future may be to recognize that its strength lies in collecting, processing, and disseminating information, not in producing a daily tonnage of newsprint. Consequently, electronic distribution may not be the threat that the newspapers think it is.

Despite the progressive aspects of media convergence, it will nonetheless contribute to the increasing pressures for change on the existing press industry. These changes in turn will put great pressure on the First Amendment to provide a constitutional definition of "the press" that will determine which media and communication entities or technologies are protected from regulatory infringement. Disputes coming to the courts will reflect the tensions erupting within the press industry as a result of these changes. And the nature of these changes will indicate the direction of future change in First Amendment press doctrines. An additional source of change will come from the introduction of even newer media technologies which will further complicate the structure and identity of the American press.

4

The Emergence of New Media Technologies

THE FORCES OF CHANGE are infiltrating the media from all directions. The emergence of new communications technologies, for instance, is greatly expanding the sphere of the press. The approaching technological transformation of the media and communications fields has been well documented, and a revolution in communications technology is occurring today that is "as profound as the invention of printing."[1] The mass media revolution is being reversed; instead of identical messages being disseminated to millions of people, electronic technology now permits the adaptation of electronic messages to the specialized or unique needs of individuals.

Dramatic new developments in electronic communications promise to radically change the way society communicates. Computer networks and bulletin boards are creating, in essence, electronic editorial pages on which people can register their viewpoints. Fiber optic cable, capable of transmitting electronic, voice, and video messages over the same cable, promises to bring customized news and information into the home over the telephone. News and information ordered over the telephone may appear on the home computer, television screen, or video phone. Television programming could even be received over the telephone lines, or perhaps direct broadcasting from satellite systems will leapfrog the present cable and emerging fiber-optic technologies as a means of providing video programming and other information services.

The upcoming technological revolution will produce new

ways of delivering information and programming. Video programming may be delivered by telephone, satellite, or cable systems. Newspapers may well evolve into some electronic format in which their contents appear on some form of computer screen or digital display. A flat-panel newspaper—a computer appliance that will look like a large note pad—can display on its screen the contents of a personal newspaper reflecting the type of special-interest information desired by the subscriber. If newspapers remain available in printed form, each subscriber's copy may be produced from their individual printers hooked up by telephone lines to the newspaper's production room. Furthermore, in receiving their own newspaper copy, subscribers may be able to customize their copy to their own particular interests.

Technological innovations are also producing new kinds of media. Teletext, for instance, can deliver hundreds of "pages" of information, including news headlines, weather reports, and stock prices from satellite or television signals to home television screens or computer monitors. Another more powerful technology is videotex—a two-way link between the television set and a central computer. By connecting directly to the data base via telephone or interactive cable, users can retrieve precisely the information they want on an almost unlimited array of subjects.

The 900-number telephone service represents another new type of interactive communications technology, and it reflects one way in which the telephone is evolving beyond person-to-person conversations and becoming a mass medium in new and interesting ways. Indeed, 900 numbers can put information and transactions at consumers' fingertips. The service promises in the future to offer valuable information and to create new information markets, such as fundraising by nonprofit organizations, general and business news, stock exchange reports, job information, access to educational services, political feedback, and public talk programs.

Electronic bulletin boards and computer networks also provide a new kind of communications forum. They have been said to be the place of "cultural chatting" in the computer age. Commercial bulletin board services like those offered by Prodigy and CompuServe have about four-and-a-half million users, and a common estimate puts the total number of bulletin board services at ten thousand.[2] One such service offered by CompuServe has

250 different forums in which subscribers can exchange information and opinions on any topic of interest to them. These "conversational" networks are immensely popular with subscribers. Both AT&T and Apple Computer have unveiled on-line systems similar to those of Prodigy and CompuServe.

Other types of informational networks have also blossomed. The largest and most well-known is the Internet, a computer network used primarily by university and government personnel, whose high-speed data lines were built by the National Science Foundation. Touted as a model for the national information superhighway, the Internet has gained popular appeal and currently has approximately twenty million users worldwide. Hundreds of schools across the country are also linked by networks such as Kids' Net which allow students to exchange electronic mail. The Telecommunications Cooperative Network, with a membership of about three thousand nonprofit organizations, offers a typically wide range of information services. Network members can broadcast urgent news and advocacy alerts to select member audiences and post information for every member to read. In another example, the Harvard Graduate School of Education has set up an electronic network for its school's graduates; approximately four thousand messages pass through the system every academic year.[3]

The experiences of CompuServe and the Telecommunications Cooperative Network also refute the fear that only computer hackers will dominate these communications forums. Moreover, polls suggest that the average person is willing to experiment with electronic information services.[4] In a 1987 Roper survey, 30 percent of respondents said they were interested in using home computers to access electronic bulletin boards and 41 percent were interested in data bases with news and other up-to-the-minute information. This willingness has translated into real growth in the electronic information business. Prodigy, which had 25,000 subscribers at the end of 1988, hit the one million mark in 1991, and had 1.75 million users by the end of 1992.

Electronic publishing in general has experienced substantial growth. This field currently covers many services: electronic mail, electronic bulletin boards, teletext (visual broadcast of pages of information), videotex (a two-way flow from the user to the computer, which stores news files or other specialized services), home shopping, and banking publications. By 1988, there were 3,699 publicly accessible on-line data bases in the United States established by 900 producers and 300 distributors. This is 3.2 times the number of data bases available in 1982, which in turn had tripled since 1979. By 1987 there were 2,546,000 subscribers to U.S. data banks, a 19 percent growth in one year.[5] Within these services, users may obtain information ranging from the most current—today's news, market quotations, entertainment schedules, or the newest journals—to longer-term information—trends, scientific theories, private or public regulations—or longest-term data—history, all-time market statistics, technical formulas, back-issue publications, legal case histories, and entertainment classics. The growth of electronic publishing has also spawned a thriving newsletter industry, which reported sales of nearly seven billion dollars in 1991 and which has grown in just a few years from only a few publications to thousands.

In addition to the new electronic publishing services, a virtually new public communications medium is close at hand, according to some media observers. Described as a national information service, it would require only modest technological enhancements to the nation's public telephone network: a smart telephone with visual display and touch-screen input capabilities; the mixing of voice, text, and graphics in a single telephone circuit connection; and installation of large-scale, computer-based network publishing systems that could receive, store, package, and, upon request, disseminate customized information to customers. This type of information service has been advocated as the public communications network of the future. Individuals could connect with this network through a new-generation telephone with a three-by-five–inch display panel. The user would be able to send and receive information from the display through a touch-screen keypad. Using the keypad, the user could request local school district information, including budget summaries and dates and agendas of board meetings, or obtain consumer information and federal agency publications from national data banks. Through national information directories, much like telephone books, users could gain access to countless information resources throughout the nation.[6]

Finally, another element of change introduced by the new media technologies lies in the emergence of innovative delivery systems. In the past, media messages have been delivered to the public through hand delivery of newspapers and reception of television signals generated by broadcast and cable systems. The future media messages, however, may come from these same delivery systems as well as from new systems such as satellite broadcasting, fiber-optic telephone lines, and electronic digitalized broadcasting. In 1992, the FCC approved a new microwave technology that could simultaneously transmit dozens of television channels through ultra high-frequency radio signals. These advanced delivery systems will not only allow new forms of information to be received, but will also greatly increase the amount of information available. Fiber-optic lines, for instance, can transmit thousands of times more traffic than can the traditional copper wire.

Although the types of new media are numerous and varied, they have certain general characteristics. One unique property of the new technologies is their interactive capability. Along with the erosion of barriers of distance and the convergence of different modes of communication into a single electronic system, a major trend in the evolution of communication technologies is their increasing interactivity. Most traditional technologies of communication are one-way and do not lend themselves to dialogue. But many of the new inventions in communication technology, such as video conferencing and electronic mail, have been designed to overcome the limitations of one-way communication. These new technologies are narrowing the gap between what were purely conversational modes, like the telephone, and what were purely one-way modes, like the television.[7]

Though the reception of mass communication is passive to a large degree, the new communications technologies are adapted to more active information seeking by the user. Indeed, a standard criticism of television revolves around the passivity of using it. The pendulum of technology, however, has begun to swing away from providing such passive media toward creating ones that permit much more vigorous interaction by the audience.[8]

The rapid rate of adoption of home computers, the tool necessary for the new interactive media of the future, roughly parallels the rate of adoption of television by U.S. households during the 1950s. Computers will allow the media of the future to be interactive rather than passive and will facilitate a shift from one-way to two-way communication. Furthermore, the emergence of interactive multimedia will bring together—on a screen in people's living rooms—information, music, voices, photographs, and video. Multimedia combines three key communications technologies: television, personal computers, and laser storage systems like the videodisc and the computer disk. Indeed, a new personal computer will merge various forms of technologies like the computer, television, and videodisc into one interactive multimedia system.[9] With such a system, the user will be able to obtain news and information simply by calling up on the screen a selection of wire-service stories, background articles, and reports from a library of videotapes or computer disks. One example of such multimedia includes a series of videodiscs from ABC News InterActive that allow users to explore subjects like the AIDS epidemic by roaming through film and video clips pulled from ABC's extensive library of news footage.

The new communications technologies like videotex and computer bulletin boards are obviously interactive by design. Yet interactive technology also promises to transform the most passive of our traditional media forms—television. Interactive television will allow people to "talk back" to their television sets by selecting programming, ordering information and entertainment fare on a pay-per-view basis, and allowing them to provide input and opinion to televised public meetings.

High-definition television (HDTV) may well achieve such interactivity. With interactive HDTV on fiber-optic cable, a television news program viewer could push the "tell me more" button on the television set and have the reporter elaborate on a particular story to various levels, providing substance that would otherwise have been relegated to the cutting-room floor.[10]

With a system of television indexing, programs could be digitally broadcast with a table of contents at the beginning. By consulting this table of contents, a programmed interactive television set could filter out inappropriate programs. It could then more or less edit the five-thousand hours of programming broadcast during a seven-hour workday into a short, distilled collage lasting no more than ten minutes. Elaborations on the subjects of interest could be obtained by request. And the personalized aspect of the provided service would be handled by the receiver, not by the network as a whole. Thus, interactive media permits the user to selectively choose and organize the information she receives, rather than simply try to absorb the content and organization of information chosen by the sender. This interactivity gives audiences more control over what they receive, permits decentralized decisions over media content, and thus creates a more fluid relationship between users and senders of information.[11]

A second general characteristic of the new media is that it increases the control over content and timing of messages, both by the receiver and the sender. By expanding the number of media, for instance, the new technologies let users select more freely among available information, and a videocassette recorder, in particular, permits viewers to program their own television sets to receive particular programs at a convenient time. Consequently, the traditional hegemony of senders—network executives, producers, editors, or publishers—increasingly erodes as the receiver exercises more discretion. The result has been a shift in sovereignty to the consumer. In a way, consumers will become coproducers of information.[12]

The new media also increase the capacity of those who send messages to determine who will get what information. Cable, for instance, can provide a wide assortment of programs tailored to particular, narrow audiences. This is commonly referred to as ''narrowcasting,'' as opposed to broadcasting. Unlike the mass media, new technology will allow publishers to tailor their messages to the interests of small specialized audiences. Furthermore, in contrast with monolithic mass media, which can only be distributed in their fixed forms, interactive two-way media may offer opportunities for cultural tuning, diversity, and multipolarity of origination that do not exist today.[13]

A third characteristic of the new media is that it promises to decentralize control over mass communications. Some media analysts believe that the new technologies foster a shift from the last three decades of centralized network television back to the historically more segmented and localized media characteristic of the American press. ''The dominance of mass media lasted a century and a half," Pool noted. "This was a unique period in human history, in which media reached the whole society. The new media in some ways restore the normal state of affairs." According to another analyst, satellites are a "democratic technology" and hold the key to a more decentralized media. Satellite transmission, for instance, has not only made cable economically viable, but has also reduced network control of broadcast television by feeding programming directly to stations.[14]

An increased decentralization of the media may also inject a more efficient sense of organization into the American communications system. The structure of the future media promises to be better organized according to the communication needs and interests of the public. People will be linked to the media not only through geography—as they are now with their local newspaper and television station—but they will also be linked according to interests and information needs. Thus, "communities of the mind" will tend to replace "communities of geography."

Some media forms will respond and cater to specific groups of individuals, and combined they will produce more information and communication roles than ever before. Not every communications technology will be a complete press in itself, unlike what newspapers once strove to be. Instead, there will be a delegation of various communication functions to different forms of media. Electronic bulletin boards and information networks will join people according to their areas of interest and involvement. Video conferencing and cable "meetings" will bring distant participants together in common ventures. On the individual level, the personalized, interactive nature of the new electronic technologies will offer individual choice of information.

The falling cost of electronic communications also supports the trend toward individualization and decentralization. Satellites and fiber links are making costs more distance-insensitive. Consequently, the communications technologies evolving today are less frozen into the uniform output of a mass medium than communications technologies of the past, and they promise to shape themselves to the needs of small audiences or individual users.[15]

The new media further contributes to decentralization by offering an opportunity for unmediated communication, bringing the public closer to the communications process by eliminating the constant buffer of the journalist. The journalist will continue to function as an information provider, but the public will be able to obtain specialized information not provided by journalists or not provided in the manner desired. Essentially, the new media will enable members of the public to communicate more directly with each other. Furthermore, as with the electronic bulletin boards, the public can also register their opinions without relying on the editor to select their letter or to edit it for publication. Thus, by including more of the public into the communication stream, the new media are similar to the eighteenth-century model of the press.

A unique feature of the electronic communication systems is the inclusion of nonjournalists in the information-sharing process. The new media are blurring the lines between news gatherer and audience and encouraging a greater nonjournalistic participation in the communication process. Rapid advances in communications technology have not only created new kinds of news delivery; they have also made it easier for individuals to compete with traditional journalists in their own medium.[16] The television program "America's Funniest Home Videos," although designed for laughs, points to a similar serious trend in television news, where we can, for example, view the Los Angeles police beating of Rodney King, captured on video by a bystander.

As journalists lose their hegemony over news and information, the new communications technologies have the potential of letting the public come closer than ever to realizing the full value of the First Amendment. After all, the whole idea behind the First Amendment was to empower people to use the news, not to make them dependent on government or a few journalists.[17]

Given these general characteristics, the new media technologies promise to make a significant contribution to the conduct of democratic politics. Indeed, changes in communications technology have often caused democratic changes in society, and modifications in the structure and technology of the press have gone hand in hand with changes in the political process. Franklin Roosevelt's use of radio, for instance, reached over the heads of Congress and journalists and made a direct contact with the electorate. Consequently, the public felt a connection to its government that it had not previously felt. Likewise, in the 1992 presidential campaign, the candidates connected with the voters through new and unprecedented media forums, such as popular talk shows and electronic town meetings. Taking advantage of various types of interactive media, the candidates sought to have more direct contact with potential voters, and the electorate responded enthusiastically. Based on this precedent, hopeful observers are optimistic that the new media will lead to a renaissance of democratic politics.[18]

One of the most powerful democratizing forces of the new technologies is their capacity for permitting interaction between the user and the sender of information. This increasing communication will hopefully lead to greater interaction of citizens in their political society. Cable "town meetings," for instance, may bring the voters in closer touch with elected officials and foster a more vibrant political dialogue. Voters with personal computers in their homes might gain access to data bases that could provide summaries about a candidate's issue stances or record.[19] As an example of the political uses of the new media, prior to the 1992 New Hampshire presidential primary, a 900-number telephone line was set up for the public to comment on or to complain about the candidates' political advertising. The aim was obviously to upgrade political campaigning by putting pressure on candidates when their ads appeared disparaging or dishonest. Furthermore, presidential candidate H. Ross Perot proposed that as president he would hold electronic town meetings in which citizens could register opinions through interactive cable television and telephone voting.[20]

A dramatic example of the political potential of the new media is found in the 1976 cable town-meeting experiment in Reading, Pennsylvania, where the new interactive capacity of television was used to overcome the social isolation of the elderly. Three neighborhood senior citizens' centers, along with the private homes of about 125 selected elderly people, were equipped with television cameras and video-recording equipment that permitted a two-way communications network. Though the program as originally designed did not call for political use of the system, it quickly became evident that senior citizens were interested in talking politics with city officials. Consequently, the daily programming soon included video-conferences with elected officials.

These video town meetings were initiated totally by the senior citizens themselves and without any outside motivation or prompting. According to one observer of this program, these televised meetings led "to the political mobilization of the entire senior community" and to the entrance of many formerly shut-in senior citizens into the political process. Thus, the new communications technologies fostered a classic model of participatory democracy.[21]

The democratic potential of the new electronic media is also illustrated by the experience of the city of Santa Monica, California. The city implemented a computer system called the Public Electronic Network (PEN), which provides electronic access to city council agendas, staff reports, public safety tips, and the public library's on-line catalog. It also allows residents to enter into electronic conferences on topics ranging from rent control to artistic events. Santa Monicans can tap into PEN from a home or office computer or use one of the public terminals in libraries and community centers. As many as sixty-four people can use the system at once, so the comments occur just as if people were sitting around a room chatting.

The motivation behind PEN was a desire to create a new kind of public meeting ground where citizens could talk to government officials and city servants on equal footing and where people could debate local political issues, free from the conventional gatekeepers in city hall and the press. More broadly, it might prove a powerful antidote to the isolation and anomie of modern urban life by offering a new way for Santa Monicans to interact and forge alliances. This, in turn, might eventually involve more residents in civic affairs. "Engagement is what democracy is all about," said Municipal Court Judge David Finkel, a member of the Santa Monica City Council in the late 1980s and an early fan of PEN. "The more people communicating on PEN, the more potential political activists there are to jump in and stir up the pot."[22]

City planners had expected the heaviest use of PEN to come from residents seeking information from one of the city's data bases. But they were wrong. From the beginning, the public conferences were by far the most popular attraction. One of the clearest lessons of PEN, according to William Dutton, a professor at the University of Southern California's Annenberg School for Communication, is that people do not crave new sources of information so much as new venues for talking to one another. Kevin McKeown, chair of the PEN Users Group, compares the system to a traditional New England town meeting, except that PEN is used on a daily basis: "It's not like writing a letter to the editor of the local newspaper, where you have a chance in a thousand that it will be published, and no one ever responds to you even if it is."[23]

Another attraction for many users is the leveling effect of the PEN conferences. Judged solely on what they communicate, people can more easily cross social barriers. Homeless people talk to the well-to-do, teenagers talk to adults, and political neophytes talk to city hall's oldest veterans. Thus, although PEN is still in its infancy and is experiencing growing pains, it may prove to be a valuable First Amendment tool. With PEN, says Jerry Mechling, director of strategic computing and telecommunications at Harvard's Kennedy School of Government, Santa Monica is "using technology to explore different ways of reaching the public."[24]

As exemplified by Santa Monica's experiment with PEN, the new press promises to support a reform or transformation of American democratic politics. Such a reform is desperately needed to reenergize democratic activism in a nation whose voting rates have plummeted and whose elected representatives have become entrenched bureaucrats. A new press that is more connected with the public may help transform politics from the confines of elected elites and powerful special interest groups back to the public. Essentially, the new press promises to support the most urgent immediate need of America's democratic system—the active involvement of the electorate.

If the media is to have a political impact, it must engage the public in political debate and inquiry; in that way only will the public truly become involved in public policy. Debate and communication is the first vital step toward political action. Consider the analogy of speeches and lectures: after a speaker delivers a lecture to a group of people—and thereby informs them—a question-and-answer session occurs in which the audience becomes more active in the subject of the lecture. The real dialogue and analysis occurs during this period. The traditional media, however, have not been able to facilitate this kind of social dialogue through the press. Yet the new media may very well rise to this task, and a participatory media is the desired outcome of the current revolution in the American press and communications systems.

In *The Electronic Commonwealth: The Impact of the New Media Technologies on Democratic Politics,* the authors examine the new media technologies' capacity for reorienting mass communications toward a more robust democratic gathering place. Their participatory vision of democracy will be supported only if the new technologies encourage collective deliberation and sustained public debates. Indeed, according to the authors—who label themselves as "agnostics" on the issue of "whether the new media constitute a communications revolution"—the new technologies do possess such potential. In fact, the authors announce that the new media offers "a better and more democratic remedy for lost citizen power" by electronically recreating the town meeting.[25]

In addition to facilitating participation in political dialogue, the new technologies also promise to support democratic pluralism. As opposed to the uniform political culture served by commercial television, for instance, cable programming has the potential to serve the many diverse needs of a pluralistic society. Narrowcast programming can protect against the majority's tendency to impose its views on all of the various minority groups in society. It can also help to preserve the voice and identity of society's collection of minority groups. Indeed, the evolving communications technologies play an important cultural role in contributing to the breakdown of social conformity. Today, the usual social criticisms of a mass-media–dominated society is that it suffers from a dull conformity where dissent and criticism have little voice. The danger of the new technologies, however, is just the opposite: that they will foster such diversity that fragmentation and social division will occur.

Of course, no one can predict precisely the effect that new media technologies will have on society or on democratic politics. In *Electronic Commonwealth,* the authors examine these new technologies and, while recognizing their positive potential, reach no conclusion on their influence on America's political health.

Yet we will never know their potential if we do not encourage their positive aspects and protect them from stunting regulations.

Despite the uncertainties of the new technologies, they do seem to offer some fairly tangible benefits. They will allow more speed in the communication process and can encourage immediate political action in response to news. Constituencies can more quickly mobilize and lobby their political representatives, and, through computer or electronic networks, the public can also make their opinions known immediately to public officials. Consequently, the new technologies may encourage the communicative and participatory function of the press, which has not operated adequately since the nineteenth century.

New communications technologies may inject more competition into a media environment that in recent decades has become increasingly monopolized. The newspaper, telephone, and cable and broadcast television industries are all beginning to compete with each other, and new forms of media technology are intensifying that competition. Microwave delivery of television programming, for instance, poses an obvious competition to cable television.

The new press—a combination of the emerging new technologies and the changing existing media—may remedy many of the traditional complaints against the press in America. It may end the monopolization and lack of diversity in the current media industry. By becoming more customized to individuals and less centralized, the new press might encourage and support regional and local cultures, which declined under the standardized mass culture of a monopolized media. News and audiences will no longer be automatically homogenized; people may no longer have to abide by a national information agenda set by a few media companies. In the past, people everywhere read and saw essentially the same news from the same few news sources.

By opening the avenues of communication to the public, the new media may enrich its role as watchdog, and it may enhance its ability to educate and inform the public. In the past, journalists have occupied the primary role of reporters of social problems. Yet in many areas journalists were largely uninformed and incompetent to educate the public. Take, for instance, the judicial system. With regard to reporting abuses or problems in that system, lawyers as well as journalists are competent and qualified informers. With a press controlled by journalists, however, lawyers perhaps felt no need or opportunity to express their views on the court system. The same could be said of environmental problems. If the new press opens up opportunities for nonjournalists like environmental engineers to express their views, the public may actually get a higher quality of information on certain environmental issues.

By reconnecting to the public, the new media may expand the size of the information audience. Newspaper readership and television viewership have declined over the last two decades. In 1970, for instance, 78 percent of U.S. adults read a newspaper each weekday. By 1990, that figure had dropped to 62 percent.[26] Among younger readers, the figures are even worse, with readership declining from 67 percent to 24 percent. (Ironically, this decline has occurred in a generation that has grown up in the age of information and that appears, at least on paper, to be the best-educated generation in history.) The new media, however, may reverse this trend by better customizing news and information to the needs and desires of the individual. Furthermore, new media such as personalized electronic newspapers, which can be programmed according to the subscribers' own information needs, will help those who feel burdened by information overload. They can, for instance, filter and sort information as well as produce and present it.

Perhaps more than any other contribution, the new media may give to the public what it has long wanted—a forum for social communication. Few individuals have been able to express their ideas and opinions on television news programs or in the editorial pages of the large metropolitan newspapers. In fostering more audience involvement, the new media may break the pattern of one-way media communication to an alienated and passive audience. It may provide a forum through which society can communicate its opinions and conduct political debate. A study of electronic networks and computer bulletin boards concluded that the successful ventures were those that facilitated the most communication among its users. Users spent far more time communicating with each other than in retrieving news.[27] The phenomenal success of CompuServe, for instance, attests to the company's vision of letting the customers dictate the information they want and the subjects of communication among them. Its growth from 1,200 customers in 1979 to 830,000 in 1991 demonstrates that the future press need not confine itself to a one-way communication flow. Observers have noted that "computer networks have created thousands of virtual communities that have been the basis for a participatory democracy, created fast friendships for millions of people."[28]

Electronic bulletin boards promise to be a great communication equalizer. Everyone can become a publisher, reporter, or editorialist, and can easily engage in public debate. This marks a significant departure from the present media, which is characterized by A. J. Liebling's observation: "Freedom of the press belongs to those who own one." Besides being far cheaper to obtain, the new electronic networks and bulletin boards differ from the traditional press in that the latter relies on a one-to-many model, while computer-based communications uses a many-to-many model. A newspaper is a typical one-to-many system: information gathering and reporting is supervised by a hierarchy of editors who control the flow of information. Computer information services, however, rely on little or no hierarchical editing. The "filtering" function performed by newspaper editors is left to the readers, who are also contributors. The very distinction between reader and reporter becomes blurred. Thus, these services resemble a town-hall meeting in which everyone has a chance to speak.

This democratic transformation of the press through the introduction of new communications technologies may result in a significant departure from the past, where the fourth estate was often quite aloof and seemingly indifferent to the communication needs and interests of nonjournalists. The approaching transformation of the press may also put democratizing pressures on the First Amendment. Yet for such changes to occur, the First Amendment will have to recognize these new technologies as "the press." And the courts will have to define "the press" as it appears in the First Amendment in order to guarantee that the democratizing influences of the new technologies will not be lost.

5

Political Pressures for a Changing Press

THE PRESS HAS CLEARLY entered a period of dramatic technological and economic change. Additional pressures for change,
however, also emanate from social and political forces. The unpopularity of the media, for instance, has fueled various reactions
against the press in both the judicial and the political arenas. In
addition, the public's distaste for contemporary "media politics"
has prompted demands for reform of the press' involvement in the
political process.

Although these pressures for change are much more ambig-
uous than those caused by the economic and technological factors
previously discussed, they may nonetheless exert a significant
influence in changing the role and identity of the American press
over the next decade. Therefore, examining these social and political pressures is necessary to understand the future direction of
change in the press.

In many respects, the political pressures for change resemble
the technological changes affecting the press. Just as many of the
new media technologies offer alternatives to an inaccessible mass
media, so also do political forces react against a mass media that
appears unresponsive to and unconcerned about the general public. Just as technology is introducing more competition into the
media, the public is turning against the monopoly power of the
traditional media. And just as the new media allows the public to
communicate without the mediated role of journalists, a restless
electorate intensifies its distrust of political reporters. Unlike the
existing media, the new technologies may create a press that

encourages public involvement and participation in the information-sharing process.

In recent decades, an inverse relationship has existed between
public opinion toward the press and the actual institutionalized
power of the press. As the press has become more concentrated,
aloof, and independent from the public, it has become more unpopular. Consequently, since the last period of significant change
in the press and in First Amendment press doctrines during the
1960s and 1970s, the public has become steadily more hostile and
suspicious toward the media. This rise in public hostility resulted
not only from the growing concentration of power in and monopolization of the media, but also from the increasingly aggressive
and adversarial journalism practiced by the press. This brand of
journalism crowded out the public from participating in the media
dialogue. Consequently, in the public's view, an aloof and abusive press became as unpopular an institution as the government
had become under President Nixon, and this trend continued into
the 1990s.[1]

The public is currently quite cynical about the "increasingly
concentrated power of the major media, suspicious of their fairness, and distressed by their wolf-pack methods of news gathering." Public respect for the press has declined, even in relation
to other unpopular social institutions. For instance, when the
media complained that the Reagan administration had prevented
it from covering the Grenada invasion, most Americans sided
with the government and believed that the media would not just
have reported the invasion but would have tried to sabotage
it. Likewise, the government's heavy-handed censorship of the
press during the Gulf War met with practically no popular resistance.[2]

The unpopularity of the press arises from several public criticisms, one of which involves the concentrated and monopolistic
nature of the media industry. Throughout this century, the media
industry has steadily concentrated ownership into substantially
fewer but larger corporations, and corporate chains have acquired
many independent and locally owned newspapers. Indeed, a
steady decline has occurred since 1940 in the number of cities
having competitive daily newspapers, with less than 4 percent of
American cities now have competing newspapers under separate

ownership. Today, more than two-thirds of all daily newspapers are owned by chains.[3]

In addition to the newspaper industry, other media groups have also become monopolized. The merger of Time, Inc. and Warner Communications, for instance, created a huge media conglomerate with interests in nearly every aspect of the communications business. Broadcast television has long been dominated by three networks; and even though cable television is fairly young, it too has become quite monopolized. Tele-Communications Inc. (TCI), the world's largest cable television company, has been criticized as "a monopolistic, strong-arm bully that squeezes other cable operators, denies free competition to programmers and flagrantly disrupts the plans of rivals."[4] In fact, the monopolistic power of TCI contributed to many calls for greater regulation of the cable industry.

This increasing monopolization and concentration in the media has inspired much criticism of the press. Ben Bagdikian, a critic of media monopolization, has outlined the adverse effects of chain-owned newspapers on the communities they serve and the censorship imposed on local editors by parent corporations. The modern monopolized press, according to Bagdikian, does not respond to the interests of local audiences; the pressure to create editorial content not for the needs and interests of the audience but to enhance advertising has greatly intensified under chain ownership.[5]

Fears of concentration of power in the media were expressed by the Commission of Freedom of the Press when it warned that a democracy could never indefinitely tolerate concentration of private power strong enough to thwart the aspirations of the people. Indeed, media concentration is perceived as a threat to American democracy and pluralism, and is seen as causing a dangerous reduction in the diversity of views disseminated through the press to the public. A recent study conducted by the American Society of Newspaper Editors revealed that more than 80 percent of independent editors thought that concentration of ownership threatens freedom of the press. Sixty-nine percent of editors of chain-owned newspapers felt the same.[6]

Further contributing to this feared reduction in viewpoints has been the relationship between a conglomerate corporate press and its advertisers. According to critics, the people who manage most media enterprises have, for many years, regarded advertisers, rather than the public, as their primary clients. For this reason, advertisers exert significant influence over media content. They have not only affected content, but have also contributed to media concentration. For instance, even in the case of single-ownership, two-newspaper cities, advertisers' abhorrence of duplicated readership has forced the widespread abandonment or merger of afternoon papers.[7]

Whatever its causes, media concentration subverts the local responsiveness of the press. Newspapers give identity to the communities where they are published, and their disappearance diminishes local civic spirit and morale. Chain ownership has drastically changed the relationship between a newspaper and its subscribing community. It has tended to make the newspaper responsive and subservient to its corporate owner than to the community that relies upon it for local news and public discourse. Instead of a fierce commitment to community, they often employ generic front pages with a televisionlike, *USA Today*-type of gloss that fits into the corporate image. According to critics, a single corporate vision gets stamped on every newspaper in the chain, and in the process a community's distinctiveness and character may be lost.[8]

The dissatisfaction with this concentrated and nonparticipatory press is reflected in the increasing barrage of libel lawsuits against the media. Although few libel suits are won against the media, those lawsuits have occurred with increasing frequency. Jury verdicts in libel cases, although usually overturned on appeal, seem to reflect the public's hostility to the press. Drawn from the public, jurors are "quite prepared to find at least reckless disregard in much of what the media do—powerful corporations shredding the reputations of comparatively defenseless individuals for profit." Consequently, libel jurors have been enthusiastic and generous in their verdicts against media defendants. Plaintiffs prevail in approximately three out of five libel trials, and punitive damages are levied in the same proportion of cases. On appeal, however, when the constitutional defense of libel law is applied, plaintiffs in libel suits succeed in less than 10 percent of cases. This disparity between trial and appeals court judgments may be explained largely by the public's animosity to the press.[9]

According to one study, the average jury verdict in public-figure defamation cases against the media in 1989 and 1990 exceeded four million dollars. Another study found average libel verdicts to be three times as high as average verdicts in medical malpractice and product liability litigation. In constant dollars, libel awards for 1980–1986 had increased more than 400 percent over the decade ending in 1964, and million-or-more-dollar awards in the same period registered a 1,000 percent increase over the previous two decades.[10]

This rash of lawsuits against the media and the corresponding increase in verdicts against it reflects a deeply ingrained hostility toward a media seemingly unaccountable and indifferent to the public. If someone feels defamed, they have no right to force the particular media organization to publish their reply. Moreover, because the public has little accessibility to or involvement in the media and because of the perception that information flowing through the press is controlled by a select group of journalists, objections about the fairness of media reporting abound. In recent years, an explosion of complaints of media bias has occurred, and these complaints come from groups ranging from ultraconservative to liberal activist, who argue that the media does not represent a cross section of America.[11]

To combat this alleged bias, media watchdog groups now exist on both the left and the right. The oldest group, however, is Accuracy in Media, a twenty-two-year-old right-wing organization headed by Reed Irvine. Yet the rising star among such groups is the Media Research Center, founded in 1987 by L. Brent Bozell III. The group is known for its scrutiny of the guest lists of programs such as "The MacNeil/Lehrer NewsHour" and "Nightline" for evidence of cultural or political bias. One study, for instance, determined that 90 percent of the nonforeign guests on "MacNeil/Lehrer" were white and 87 percent were male.[12]

Conflicting studies have also documented the alleged biases and unfairness of the media. Media critic Ben Bagdikian, for instance, maintains that the media is controlled by a few giant corporations and that it expresses and supports the interests of these corporations. Conservative critics, however, claim that the press is dominated by a "liberal media elite" who choose sources and select reportable information that generally matches their own liberal orientation.[13] These journalists, according to critics, not only place a liberal bias on the news but also inject an antagonism to traditional values and institutional authority. Studies conducted after the 1992 presidential election, even by the nonpartisan Freedom Forum Media Studies Center, concluded that journalists are more likely to identify with the Democratic party than the general public does. Likewise, polls conducted by the Times Mirror Center for the People and the Press found that voters also sensed a journalist bias against George Bush and a favoritism toward Bill Clinton.[14]

In general, the public has expressed concerns and complaints about media fairness. One recent study found that 42 percent of the public thought the president of the United States ought to be able to close down a newspaper that he felt was biased or inaccurate. And according to surveys between 1985 and 1989 by the Times Mirror Center for the People and the Press and the Gallup organization, a majority of Americans believed that the press as a whole was biased and negative, as well as influenced by powerful organizations and unwilling to admit mistakes. A 1984 credibility study by the American Society of Newspaper Editors found that 75 percent of those surveyed believed reporters were only concerned about getting a good story and had no worry about hurting people.[15] Moreover, a survey conducted by the *Columbia Journalism Review* revealed the divergent views of journalists and the public regarding the manner in which the news is reported. According to the results, 77 percent of the press thinks it deals fairly with all sides of the issues, whereas only 28 percent of the public thinks so; and 66 percent of the journalists think they are willing to admit to mistakes, but only 34 percent of the public think they are. In trying to explain this disparity of opinions and why the public views the press with such mistrust, journalists have recognized that "the public completely misunderstands what we do," and that they "do not explain ourselves enough, and thus are seen as mysterious, arrogant, and unapproachable." Indeed, these statements show how disconnected the press has become from the public.[16]

As another reflection of the hostility between the press and the public, invasion of privacy complaints against the media are on the rise. Editors have reported significant increases in privacy complaints from the public. A 1985 study found that more than half the editors surveyed had recently changed their policies on identifying crime victims, toward using less personal detail, and a January 1990 Harris poll reported that 79 percent of Americans felt their personal privacy was threatened by the press. To guard individual privacy from the media, a growing number of states have proposed or enacted legislation that limits the type of information that the press can publish on crime victims.[17]

As a result of the rising concerns with privacy, regulatory precautions are being taken against some of the new telecommunications technologies. In the Telephone Consumer Protection Act of 1991, for instance, Congress enacted measures that permit consumers to block calls from various kinds of salespeople. State legislatures have also become involved in regulating telephone privacy. Several states have enacted regulations for proposed caller-identification services.[18] These regulations reflect the fear that caller identification could dramatically increase the number of intrusive calls into the home and that through the use of reverse directories businesses could use a caller's telephone number to obtain a person's name and address as well. Because of these privacy concerns, the FCC has similarly initiated a rule-making process to develop federal standards in this area.

As with the other aspects of the current media unpopularity, privacy concerns have resulted from the perception that the press only "intrudes" and rarely "involves." The media's somewhat visible focus on investigative, adversarial journalism has given it the image of a social predator preying upon a helpless public. Moreover, as the United States increasingly becomes more of a media society and with the public having little control over social dialogue through the press, social problems publicized by the media often get blamed, however unfairly, on the messenger—a phenomenon that further intensifies public dissatisfaction with the media.

Of all the complaints against the media, perhaps none are quite as intense as those concerning the media's role in politics. A consistent and fundamental complaint is that the modern media allows for virtually no participation by the general public and gives the journalist an exclusive role in the information-sharing process. In the political sphere, the exclusion of the public from social dialogue through the media is believed to cause a corresponding citizen withdrawal from the political process itself. Lately, almost all of the ills of American politics have been attributed to the press. Therefore, many of the efforts to reform the political process have focused on changing the media's role.

It is obviously impossible to analyze the modern political process without considering the powerful and sometimes degenerative impact of the media. Politics experienced through television has become a one-way activity—it permits no direct input from the public. Instead of making politics more of a communal exercise, television appears to have had the reverse effect. Indeed, this reverse effect contradicts much of the American historical experience with the press.

Eighteenth-century U.S. newspapers were normally read and discussed in social settings. In the nineteenth century, newspapers were highly partisan organs used by the political parties to help in turning elections into rituals of group solidarity. During the past thirty years, however, television has helped shift democracy away from a group event to an atomized and essentially passive experience. Although Alexis de Tocqueville once observed that the American press brought people together, helped politicize the issues, and contributed to the formation of public opinion, the modern media often does the opposite—it treats politics as a spectator sport. News organizations "rarely go beyond treating the public as consumer"; and even when journalism seeks to educate, the public role "is still likely to be conceived as passive."[19]

As much as the modern media has improved the quality of its investigative reporting, it has abandoned its function of providing a forum for social and political dialogue among the public. By becoming a mass media with a largely standardized informational product, the existing press has lost its historical connection with the public; it has become less and less an interactive forum in which the public can initiate its involvement in politics.

By emphasizing investigative reporting and scandal coverage, the press has largely ignored the marketplace function, which is the provision of a forum for public participation in social debate and dialogue. Not surprisingly, the current decline of popular participation in the political process reflects a passive public in the communications process. Unfortunately, the modern corporate press offers little opportunity to engage the public in active communication. Instead, an increasingly passive public sits before the television night after night taking in the news without any opportunity to share views on that news or to debate opinions about it.

The "insider approach" taken by the media in its campaign coverage contributes to the public's alienation from the media and the political process. This insider approach, focusing on a small number of experts, has turned ordinary voters into outsiders, especially in connection with television news. Dan Hallin's research indicates that, in 1972, preelection evening news broadcasts used ordinary voters in more than 20 percent of the sound bites, but by 1988 that share had dropped to 3 to 4 percent—and then they were used "almost exclusively to illustrate poll results, not to contribute ideas to the campaign coverage." Thus, it is hardly surprising that citizens are having trouble identifying with campaigns and their coverage.[20]

The insider's perspective taken by the media also focuses on the most obvious and enticing part of the campaign: the horse-race drama of which candidate is likely to win. Indeed, poll-based journalism in political coverage has grown steadily. During the month prior to the 1988 election, for instance, the *Washington Post* ran thirteen poll stories on its front page and the *New York Times* ran ten, or an average of one poll story on the front page every three days.[21] Horse-race coverage also leads to more stories about campaign strategy than about substance and inevitably prompts the press to turn increasingly to so-called "spin doctors" for analysis of campaign events. The use of such spin doctors, however, perpetuates the media's insider approach to politics.

This insider approach has been blamed as a leading cause of voter apathy. A Kettering Foundation report, for instance, concluded that an unprecedented number of Americans felt alienated from politics. Many critics have blamed the drop to fifty percent of Americans voting in presidential elections to the quality of political dialogue presented through the media. In its report, the

Kettering Foundation suggests that voter alienation is due to the media's failure to involve the people in political discourse and debate. Similarly, Curtis Gans of the Committee for the Study of the American Electorate has concluded that "the principal causes of continued low and declining voter participation . . . lies not in voting laws and procedures, not in mobilization and demography, but in the quality and content of our politics." According to Gans, low voter participation is a direct result of the media's encouragement of a passive public as political spectators.[22]

The media's reliance on sound bites in its political coverage has also contributed to voter apathy and has diminished the quality of political discourse and the public's involvement in that discourse. Dan Hallin and Kiku Adatto found that the average sound bite, or bloc of uninterrupted speech by presidential candidates on the network evening news, had shrunk from 42.3 seconds in 1968 to 9.8 seconds during the 1988 campaign, thus demonstrating how television's addiction to rapid-fire sound bites and pictures has dramatically changed our political discourse. "Naturally, nothing of any significance is going to be said in 9.8 seconds," said Walter Cronkite. Critics have complained about this trend ever since it began, but never as much as today. NBC's Tom Brokaw recently bemoaned "the cancer of the sound bite" afflicting presidential campaigning.[23]

The increasingly adversarial role taken by the modern press in the last several decades has also contributed to the public's mistrust of the political process itself. As the media has focused on acting as a watchdog on government and public officials, campaign coverage has centered on exposing the faults and weaknesses of candidates. Consequently, stories about gaffes and scandals have often replaced a discussion of social issues. According to Suzanne Garment, the press has placed corruption at the very center of its concerns and has thus permitted scandals to dominate political discourse at the expense of stories of more complex social importance that, for instance, made Americans aware of the savings and loan crisis. This incessant scandal-dominated public dialogue has caused a steep rise in the political alienation of a public that has come to completely distrust anything government does.[24]

In addition to the increasing emphasis on scandal journalism, the physical presence of the press in modern political campaigns tends to crowd out public dialogue on the issues. The sheer physical staging necessary to produce visually potent events for a large press corps tends to distance local observers, physically, from the campaigning candidates. Thus, even the contemporary equivalents of a whistle-stop trip leave those who actually come to see the candidate with a sense of distance and alienation—the feeling of being an extra in a feature film production. For example, when Bill Clinton appeared in Concord, New Hampshire, during the 1992 primary campaign and found the throngs of journalists interposed between himself and the people, he remarked, "The voters don't have a chance."[25]

Many of the criticisms of media politics were reflected in postelection observations of the 1988 presidential campaign. Political analysts lamented the absence of dialogue on the urgent and substantial issues. Because of the focus on the sex life of Gary Hart, the plagiarism of Joseph Biden, the personal background of Dan Quayle, and the negative advertising aimed at Michael Dukakis, many political observers argued that the electorate was cheated of its chance to consider the issues of substance. Voters had barely any exposure to the real problems facing the nation and went through an election season largely unenlightened by any serious discussion of issues. Not surprisingly, this decline of political discourse was blamed on the media. A Gallup poll conducted in October 1988, for instance, found that voters, by a three-to-one margin, considered the campaign more negative than past contests and blamed the news media's coverage more than the campaign managers or the candidates themselves. Similarly, a public opinion poll taken after the 1988 campaign by the Times-Mirror Center for the People and the Press showed that the press had been given a D+ grade for its role in the campaign—the lowest grade received among the campaign participants, the political parties, pollsters, and even campaign consultants.[26]

Because of all the problems with and public hostility toward the traditional press and its role in the political process, candidates in the 1992 presidential election increasingly turned to "the new media" to reach voters. This new media included cable television, infotainment talk shows like "Larry King Live" and "Donahue," computer bulletin boards, 800 numbers, and satellite hookups. Candidates found that the new interactive media "gives people a sense that they have a direct role in the political process." Contrary to the "old media" of network television and large newspapers, the new media is unmediated—it allows candidates and voters to talk without any filtering by journalists. In their postelection analyses, political observers theorized that 1992 would "be remembered as the year that the mainstream political press lost control." They also credited the new media with "galvanizing U.S. voters [and] making them much more interested in the process. Consequently, the campaigns of Bill Clinton and Ross Perot used "new technologies [such as 800 numbers and computer networks] to bypass traditional news outlets whenever possible."[27]

The rising popularity of the interactive new media hs intensified social pressures to reform the mainstream press and its role in politics. These pressures in many respects coincide with the changes being introduced by the technological developments and regulatory reforms in the media. In general, all these pressures for change tend to make the media more accessible, participatory, and conducive to social dialogue.

Yet the unpopularity of the press will not only contribute to pressures for changes in the press, it will also put added pressure on First Amendment press doctrines. Unfortunately, the complaints against the media's role in politics has translated into opposition to the First Amendment, which is seen to protect the media in that role. Though the First Amendment was originally given to the people as a protection against the government, it has now come to be perceived as the weapon of the press against the public and as a special protection for monopolistic media corporations and abusive journalists. Furthermore, as it protects a press which has been blamed for many of the faults of the political process, the First Amendment becomes in perception less relevant to democratic society and perhaps even destructive to democratic processes.

First Amendment press freedoms, however, cannot long endure as antagonists to democracy. Indeed, under the theory that a democracy can be maintained only through free speech, democratic values provided the rationale for the expansion of First Amendment protections in the twentieth century.[28] Thus, the future vitality of First Amendment press freedoms may depend on their support and incorporation of democratic values. And the changing press provides an opportunity to reshape First Amendment press doctrines in a way that more strongly supports democratic processes. Spurred on by the democratic potential of the new media technologies, the approaching changes in First Amendment doctrines may protect a press that will better serve the public's political communication and democratic participation needs.

An insight into the next change in First Amendment press doctrines, however, requires an understanding of the existing doctrines. Those doctrines, established during the 1960s and 1970s, have in many ways set the stage for the upcoming changes in the application of the First Amendment press clause.

■ PART III ■

The Need for Change in First Amendment Press Doctrines

*A changing press will put pressures on existing First Amend-
ment doctrines to redefine the nature and identity of the constitutionally protected press. This definition will require new First
Amendment doctrines because the current doctrines are not
capable of accommodating the approaching changes in the
press; nor can they protect the special interactive characteristics of the new media technologies.*

*The only existing constitutional model and view of the press
arose during the 1970s—the last period of First Amendment
change. The fourth estate model has significantly influenced
First Amendment press law for the last couple of decades.
Though this model fit the needs and structure of the press in
the 1970s, it is ill equipped for the rapidly changing press of
the 1990s. Furthermore, the fourth estate model has come under much criticism recently and actually seems to have contributed to many of the current complaints against the political
role of the media.*

6

The Existing Constitutional Model of the Press

The First Amendment Revolution of the 1960s

THE PRESS HAS existed in America since almost a century before the Revolutionary War with England. Freedom of the press was constitutionally protected when the First Amendment was ratified in 1791. During the nineteenth century, a robust press greatly influenced the nature of American society and politics; names like Hearst and Pulitzer stand out in the history of their time. Yet not until the 1960s did the courts give any serious independent consideration to the First Amendment's free press clause, apart from the free speech clause.

Until the 1970s, little thought had been given to the notion that the press clause created any rights or freedoms separate from those guardeded by the speech clause. The First Amendment was viewed as protecting a general freedom of expression, without regard to whether the expression occurred between individuals or through the press. In the 1960s and 1970s, however, the press began bringing to the courts certain cases involving its own unique activities and interests, and in the course of adjudicating these cases, the courts and the press began to formulate a view of the First Amendment press clause that stood apart from that of the speech clause.

During this time, a wave of First Amendment cases pounded the courts. The cases reflected the social and political turmoil of the time. In a society struggling to break free of old patterns of deference and authority, an aggressive and questioning press soon

75

found itself in the midst of judicial conflict over its rights and activities. Many of the cases focused on the journalism practices of the press. Mirroring the public's concern for more openness in government, the press sought constitutional powers to investigate government and to gather news free of political interference. As it battled the government over access to information, particularly in its reporting of Watergate and Vietnam, the press took on an adversarial posture. The judicial conflicts between the press and the government reflected this relationship, in which the government sought to control the reporting activities of journalists and the press sought greater constitutional power and independence from government. Of particular interest, for instance, was the freedom from government compulsion to identify confidential news sources. Indeed, as the press became more aggressive in its investigations, the government in turn attempted to use the press as a source of information, subpoenaing journalists to testify about their sources. As the press opposed such measures, the disputes between the press and the government quickly rose to the Supreme Court.

The Press' Litigation Strategy to
Obtain Special Rights

To accommodate its new adversarial posture, the press in such cases as *Branzburg v. Hayes,* 408 U.S. 665 (1972), and *Richmond Newspapers, Inc. v. Virginia,* 448 U.S. 555 (1980), attempted to strengthen its newsgathering powers and its access to government information. In other cases, the press sought special rights to insulate itself from hostile attacks from either the government or private individuals who were unhappy with its aggressive reporting. The prior restraint cases protected the press from government censorship, while the libel cases protected the press from the public and the censorship effects of libel lawsuits.[1]

In all these cases, however, the consistent theme was the press' striving for judicial recognition as a special institution with distinctive rights. Although courts were highly reluctant to grant to the press any rights and freedoms not enjoyed by the general public, the press was somewhat successful in its efforts to obtain some special constitutional status. In *First National Bank of Boston v. Bellotti,* 435 U.S. 765 (1978), for instance, Justice Lewis Powell agreed that the press had a special and constitutionally recognized role: "The press cases emphasize the special and constitutionally recognized role of that institution in informing and educating the public, offering criticism, and providing a forum for discussion and debate." However, Chief Justice Warren Burger, in his concurring opinion, stated that the "Court has not yet squarely resolved whether the press clause confers upon the institutional press any freedom from government restraint not enjoyed by all others." One difficulty with interpreting the press clause as conferring special status on the press, according to Burger, was in defining the press—a task that still remains to be done.

Although the courts have not yet adequately defined the press, some decisions suggest that the courts do at times treat the press as a special institution with special rights. In *Minneapolis Star and Tribune Co. v. Minnesota Commissioner of Revenue,* 460 U.S. 575 (1983), a newspaper company sought repeal of a "use tax" on the cost of paper-and-ink products used in the printing process. The tax, however, applied only to those newspapers whose costs exceeded $100,000. The Court held that the ink-and-paper tax violated the First Amendment not only because it singled out the press, but also because it targeted a small group of newspapers. Thus, unlike other businesses in other industries, the press cannot be singled out for the imposition of special or different taxes.

The press has also received special consideration in its distribution activities, such as news rack placement. In *Lakewood v. Plain Dealer Publishing Co.,* 108 S.Ct. 2138 (1988), the Court invalidated a local news rack ordinance that gave discretion to public officials to determine news rack placement, even though the city had attempted to distinguish the ordinance as a business regulation of general application. Yet no other business or industry received such beneficial treatment in its marketing and distribution activities. The press has therefore been somewhat successful in obtaining at least an occasional judicial recognition of special status.

The Fourth Estate Model of the Press

In its quest for special constitutional protection, the press espoused a particular view of the First Amendment that would justify its sought-after freedoms and privileges. Called the "fourth estate" view, it emphasized the role of the press as one of alerting the public to abuses and incidents of corruption in government. This watchdog role is served when the press discovers and disseminates information about conditions otherwise kept from public view or which are unlikely to be discovered except by the press.

Justice Potter Stewart advocated a constitutional theory of the free press clause that was constructed primarily upon this watchdog value. According to Justice Stewart, the primary purpose of the free press clause is to create a "fourth estate" outside the government to serve as an additional check on the three official branches. Justice William O. Douglas also expressed this view when he stated that "the function of the press is to explore and investigate events, inform the people what is going on, and to expose the harmful as well as the good influences at work."[2]

Vincent Blasi provided the theoretical foundation for the watchdog or checking value theory of the First Amendment press clause. Blasi saw this function as distinct from the self-governing role of the First Amendment as proposed by Alexander Meiklejohn. According to Meiklejohn, the framers enacted the First Amendment to ensure the dissemination of the kind of information required for enlightened self-government. Self-government is supported, according to Meiklejohn, when the public is able to share ideas, determine truth, and participate in the democratic dialogue on public issues.[3]

Under Blasi's theory, the public has a more passive role in the stream of political communication than it had under Meiklejohn's theory. According to Blasi, the role of the ordinary citizen is not so much to contribute on a continuing basis to the formation of public policy as to retain a veto power to be employed when the decisions of officials pass certain bounds. He believes that the Meiklejohn view of the First Amendment as essentially protecting individual democratic decision making is outmoded. To Blasi, the vision of active and continued involvement by citizens fails to describe the reality of American politics. Protection of the media, rather than protection of the citizens' ability to participate in democratic dialogue and decision making (as espoused by Meiklejohn), became the fundamental First Amendment objective under the fourth estate model. Journalists, and not the citizenry, were seen as the essential "check" on government excess. The individual citizen was perceived to be remote and helpless, at least when compared to the two major protagonists—government and the media.

Not surprisingly, the fourth estate theory of the press followed in the wake of the shift toward adversarial investigative journalism that took place in the 1960s. This shift most notably occurred during Vietnam and Watergate, when the press became deeply antagonistic and combative toward a government perceived to be secretly acting against the interests of the public. As a result, journalists came to believe that government could not be trusted.[4]

The growth of the radical and counterculture movements also led to an adversarial relationship between press and government. As the press reported about the often illegal activities of these radical groups, law enforcement officials found journalists to be tempting sources of information. Consequently, a wave of subpoenas and law enforcement investigations aimed at the press left journalists with the attitude that government wanted to cut off their flow of information. As a result, many journalists viewed cooperation with law enforcement authorities as a threat to their ability to investigate.

The fourth estate view supported the press in its news-gathering cases. It focused on the freedoms and activities of journalists, rather than on the public as a whole. Under this view, journalists would serve as agents of the public in checking an inherently abusive government. To empower it to fulfill such a role, the press had to possess special rights to gather news. Thus, under the fourth estate model, a free press was essentially equated with a powerful press, which possessed special privileges of news gathering.

This view of the press came to be quite popular, as seen in the news-gathering cases of the 1970s, and it still continues to shape the identity of the press. For instance, the characterization of the press as a watchdog appears frequently in journalism literature. Journalism texts refer to the press as the ''fourth estate'' and the press and reporters as ''independent watchdogs.'' Judicial recognition of the importance of the press' watchdog function also finds expression in First Amendment case law. In *Sheppard v. Maxwell,* Justice Thomas Clark wrote, ''The press . . . guards against the miscarriage of justice by subjecting the police, prosecutors and judicial processes to extensive public scrutiny.'' Justice Hugo Black, in *New York Times v. United States,* wrote that ''the press was protected so that it could bare the secrets of government and inform the people.'' And in *Saxbe v. Washington Post Company,* 417 U.S. 843 (1974), Justice Lewis Powell called the press ''an agent of the public at large.''[5]

Despite this general agreement and support for a watchdog role of the press, however, the fourth estate model has received inconsistent and hesitant treatment in the courts, largely because the courts have not wanted to create unqualified affirmative rights of news gathering under the First Amendment. For instance, while recognizing that news gathering was entitled to some constitutional protection, because ''without some protection for seeking out the news freedom of the press could be eviscerated,'' the Court in *Branzburg v. Hayes* (665, 681) narrowly restricted that protection. Since *Branzburg,* the Court has failed to develop a consistent stance toward a right of news gathering. While it has recognized a First Amendment right to gather news, it has refused to enforce it in various situations. Furthermore, the *Branzburg* decision has subsequently been given almost as many interpretations as there have been lower courts construing it. Such interpretations range from conclusions that it precludes creation of a journalist's privilege, to determinations that it allows lower courts to devise such a privilege, to assertions that *Branzburg* itself recognizes a privilege.[6]

Aside from the matter of the degree of its judicial acceptance, the fourth estate theory remains the most accepted comprehensive model of the press and of the First Amendment press clause. This model grew out of the particular needs of the existing press industry in the 1970s and out of the changes experienced by that industry during the preceding years. A changing press and the disputes it spawned gave birth to the fourth estate theory. In turn, this theory significantly contributed to the changes in First Amendment press doctrines during the 1960s and 1970s.

Changes in the Press that Led to
the Fourth Estate Model

The fourth estate theory was fashioned from a press industry that by the 1960s had greatly changed. It had come to be dominated by large, powerful corporations ready and able to battle government. Perhaps most of all it was a press that had become committed to adversarial journalism.

The mass media in the 1960s and 1970s consisted primarily of corporations that were rapidly consolidating and increasing in monopolistic power. In the newspaper industry, for instance, competition had been replaced by consolidation. From 1910 to 1968, the number of cities with commercially competing dailies declined from 689 to 45. And from 1923 to 1973, the percentage of newspapers facing direct competition from another newspaper declined from 60 percent to 5 percent. Indeed, in the 1970s, twenty corporations controlled more than half the sixty-one million daily newspapers sold each day.[7]

This growth in the corporate identity of the newspaper industry influenced the direction of First Amendment press doctrines. One such influence occurred in the law of libel. As newspapers became large organizations with layers of authority and responsibility, the increased complexity of the editorial process complicated the legal issues arising in libel litigation. Publishers, editors, correspondents, and "news-collectors" all had a hand in generating the news. Consequently, there were greater chances of mistakes being made in the editorial process; and, in order to aggressively report the news, publishers wanted the freedom to make mistakes. Therefore, they began arguing that libel law should be changed to account for the peculiarity of their profession, and this change occurred in *New York Times v. Sullivan*.[8]

Along with the increased concentration in the media, there also occurred a greater sense of professional identity among journalists employed by the media chains. This increasing professionalization likewise contributed to pressures for adoption of fourth estate views. Although the journalism profession had first taken

root during the "professionalization" period of the early twentieth century, a strong sense of professionalism in the press did not
take hold until the postwar period. By the 1960s the journalism
profession had begun to mature, and professional journalists occupied all levels of the media chain of organization. With a keener
sense of identity and independence, journalists began to craft the
art of investigative reporting. Perhaps more than at any other time
in history, journalists and the press not only saw investigative
reporting as their duty, but also as an exciting endeavor.

Investigative reporting exploded in the era of Vietnam and
Watergate. Suddenly, investigative journalists had become superstars and heroes in their profession and to the public at large. The
movie *All the President's Men*, for instance, depicted reporters
Bob Woodward and Carl Bernstein as heroic crusaders, and it
reflected a period of great adulation of investigative reporters.

Not only did the development of the journalism profession in
general and investigative journalism in particular contribute to the
adversarial stance of the press during the 1970s, but the actions of
the government seemed to demand such a stance. The adversarial
stance of the press reflected a cynical presumption that government would not only fail to tell the truth but would practice
widespread deception. Consequently, the press was the only institution that could be believed and trusted to tell the truth. This
deep mistrust of government combined with journalists' own
groping for professional identity to produce the adversarial journalism of the 1960s and 1970s. With journalists more combative
toward the government, the media increasingly found itself in
court.

The First Amendment cases coming to the Supreme Court
during the 1960s and 1970s reflected this adversarial journalist
focus. The cases tended to involve journalistic activities, such as
news-gathering rights and privileges to maintain confidential
sources. Similarly, after passage of the Freedom of Information
Act in 1966 and its amendment in 1974, the press brought a
barrage of cases against the government demanding access to
information under the act.[9] The Federal Open Meetings Law also
prompted demands from the press for access to various public
records and government meetings, and these demands often resulted in litigation.

In short, the vast majority of press cases coming to the courts in the 1960s and 1970s resulted from the press' transformation to a more adversarial, investigative, and journalist-controlled press. The change in media structure to a more monopolistic and concentrated industry not only tended to remove it somewhat from the public, but also empowered it to do battle with government. Indeed, with regard to the print press, no First Amendment decision focused on the public's involvement with or interest in the press. The Court has even held that the public does not have any right of access to the print press, no matter what newspapers printed and no matter how monopolistic those newspapers were.

The fourth estate view of the press evolved out of the press cases of the 1970s. Although the courts never specifically intended to define "the press," the case law, for the first time, articulated the kind of press protected by the constitution. Essentially, the fourth estate view sought to describe the type of journalistic activities covered by the First Amendment. Under that view, the press and the First Amendment became tied to a specific class of persons—journalists exposing government corruption and abuse.

Although the fourth estate theory was an initial attempt to understand the press clause, it is now up to the future First Amendment cases to better clarify the constitutional meaning of the press. Furthermore, the fourth estate view has lately become quite unpopular. Indeed, as tensions rise between the interests of journalists and the communication interests of the public, the fourth estate model draws increasing criticism. Consequently, by the early 1990s, the courts had somewhat pulled back from the fourth estate stances they took in the 1970s. Because of this demise in the fourth estate model—the only real existing constitutional model of the press—it will become ever more imperative to reach a new definition of the press that protects the new media technologies and the functions they serve in addition to the traditional watchdog role of the press.

7

The Inadequacy of Existing First Amendment Models

THE FOURTH ESTATE VIEW of the press never evolved out of an independent effort by the courts to define the press. It developed in the courtroom battles over the rights of the press, not in the thoughtful environment of philosophers.[1] Born out of litigation, the fourth estate view essentially arose from the type of industry the press had become and from the kind of journalistic activities the press had pursued. In the cases coming to the courts during the 1960s and 1970s, the focus was on what the press was doing, not on what it was. And even though the fourth estate view received inconsistent support from the Supreme Court, it was the only overall view of the press offered in the courts and widely accepted by the media.

The fourth estate model is still the only constitutional view of the press that has any significant support. Yet this support is eroding, especially as the fourth estate model attracts increasing criticism. Furthermore, it appears incapable of resolving the First Amendment press disputes that will be coming to the courts as the result of a dramatically changing press industry. It also may be unable to take advantage of the opportunity afforded by new media technologies to expand press freedoms beyond the journalistic focus they now have under the fourth estate model, since it neither recognizes nor protects an interactive and participatory press. Consequently, during the approaching period of change in the press and in the First Amendment press doctrines, the latter must evolve beyond those articulated by the fourth estate model.

The time has come to move away from a fourth estate model

of the First Amendment not only because that model appears inadequate for the future, but also because it has proved to be inadequate in the past. Indeed, the fourth estate model actually seems to accentuate many of the faults of the existing mass media. Perceived as strengthening an already too-powerful press, the fourth estate view highlights the monopoly power of the press; focusing on the special news-gathering rights of journalists, it accents the aloofness of the press from the public; and strengthening the press against attacks by libel and privacy suits, the fourth estate view exaggerates the lack of any meaningful public access to the media.

Not only does the fourth estate model exaggerate the most unpopular aspects of the modern media, but it also takes an overly narrow view of the press as primarily an investigative watchdog over government. By ignoring the press' role in providing a social communication forum, the fourth estate model reveals its inability to protect the new press technologies which focus on providing such a forum. Indeed, much of the opposition to the fourth estate view of the press has centered on its failure to incorporate or consider the public's interest in communicating through the press. Simply giving newspapers special immunity from legal action, for instance, is not equivalent to enhancing the right of free expression for all members of the community. Furthermore, as media outlets become consolidated into fewer corporations, the press becomes even less responsive to or representative of the public. This criticism has been made by Justice Byron White, who opposed the fourth estate role of the press on the grounds that the goals of the monopolized press and the public interest are not always synonymous.[2]

The fourth estate model effectively enhances and magnifies the power of some of the participants in the communications process—particularly, the owners of the mass media and their journalist employees—with apparently no thought as to whether that power will actually enlarge and protect the public's opportunities for expression.[3] In strengthening and isolating the press from the public, however, the fourth estate model conflicts with the increasing diversity and pluralism of American society. Furthermore, the fourth estate model primarily focuses upon the public as a passive audience rather than as active participants in the communication process. It favors the interests of the audience to hear over the individual's interest or opportunity to participate in public discussions. Consequently, a fourth estate press has failed to provide a communication channel for society. As the press has become more focused on providing an information channel for journalists to educate the public, it has virtually ignored any role in engaging the public in a democratic dialogue or in encouraging the input of the average citizen. Essentially, the press has become a one-way communication stream—from the journalists to a passive audience.

By almost exclusively emphasizing investigative journalism, the fourth estate model has also ignored the role opinion plays in a democratic society, the importance of which is discussed in depth in chapter 10. Although existing as unchallenged monopolies, most newspapers today seem to have little character of their own and reflect no real viewpoint or identity of the region. Whereas opinion used to be the central ingredient of early newspapers, the modern media's obsession with so-called objectivity has shunned any effort to present strong opinions. Yet the new media may bring opinions back into the media dialogue. In December 1993, a cable channel named National Empowerment Television became the nation's first public affairs television channel with a declared ideological (conservative) spin.

In addition to a relative lack of concern with opinion, the fourth estate model rests on several myths perpetuated by journalists in the First Amendment press cases of the 1960s and 1970s. The first myth was that any right of access would destroy a free press—the argument made in *Miami Herald Publishing Co. v. Tornillo* (1974). No right was given, yet a subsequently disgruntled public came to increasingly sue the press for libel. The press is now claiming that the rising cost of defending libel litigation is destroying a free press.

Another myth promised that a fourth estate press could adequately represent society because it would present the news in an objective, fair, and unbiased manner. Yet in recent years the mass media has been beset by complaints from all kinds of groups who claim that the news is neither balanced nor fair nor unbiased. Furthermore, the recent surge of ethical complaints against the practices of the press, including plagiarism and fabrication of facts, reveals that journalists are vulnerable to mistakes and ill intentions.

The third myth fostered by journalists was that investigative and adversarial reporting deserves special protection because it is far more important to a democratic society than the dissemination of opinion. Yet much of the current political decay relates more to an absence of public opinion and discourse than from an insufficient amount of investigative reporting. Furthermore, one of the primary causes of the current political crisis is the high level of voter apathy and alienation, rather than the lack of information on certain issues of public policy. While the fourth estate model seeks to improve the latter, it virtually ignores the former.

A final myth upon which the fourth estate view rested was that the press served as an agent of the public and could adequately cover all the issues of importance. Yet minority groups are now claiming that the press is not only failing to act as their agent, but that the media is unfairly depicting them in a negative light and not covering the issues significant to them. Furthermore, the press continues to miss major stories not because it is legally prevented from pursuing those stories, but because it fails to see the importance of those stories.

The Gulf War also showed the weakness of the press-as-agent claim. During that war, the press dedicated nearly all its resources to covering what it wanted to cover—that is, the military conduct of the war in the Middle East—rather than covering what the public needed to know in terms of its own political needs—the cost of the war, the impact on the budget, and future conservation plans to lessen the country's dependence on foreign oil. Nothing arouses people from their political apathy more quickly than being personally touched by a public policy. Yet the media never encouraged or presented a discussion of what the government and the public could do to fight the war—such as a gas tax—even though, according to one poll, 54 percent of the respondents thought it would be necessary to raise taxes to pay for the war.[4] The media never fully facilitated a public dialogue about the political ramifications and implications of the Gulf War. By embracing the patriotic fervor of the war, however, the press also tended to undermine its credibility as a check or watchdog on government. Indeed, the media seemed more like military cheerleaders than the watchdogs on government envisioned by the fourth estate model.

Perhaps the most serious criticism of the fourth estate model involves the political role it creates for the media. The exclusive focus of the fourth estate model upon the adversarial and watchdog function of the press, though made with the intent of improving the workings of government, instead may have weakened the democratic foundations of our political system. Contrary to the fourth estate model, which envisions the press as informing a primarily passive audience, there is an increasing thrust toward having the press serve as a mechanism for achieving greater citizen communication and political participation.[5] This participatory press would seek to counteract the political apathy and passivity—as well as the decline of political discourse—among the public. Such a participatory press, however, is not found in the fourth estate model. Yet it may be the only kind of press truly supportive of a democratic society. And it is the kind of press that many of the new media technologies promise to achieve.

The health of a democracy depends on public involvement in political activities, such as voting, which in turn depends largely on participation in the communicative process. The fourth estate model, however, holds that the health of a democracy depends upon the press' ability to check and expose government. It does not recognize the social values of communication, nor does it answer or even address the problem of voter apathy occurring during periods of a dominant focus on adversarial journalism. Indeed, the danger of an exclusive fourth estate function for the press lies in the tendency of an adversarial, concentrated press to abandon its role of providing a forum for social communication.

By conventional reasoning, one might have anticipated that the expansion of the First Amendment in the 1970s would have led to a flowering of ideas with a consequent enrichment of American political culture. To the contrary, however, U.S. political culture has deteriorated and is presently awash in a crisis of apathy, cynicism, and ignorance. In the 1988 election, for instance, voter turnout was 50.2 percent, the lowest in sixty-four years. Turnout rates in off-year elections are even lower: in 1986, it was 37.6 percent, the lowest since 1942. Many critics see a connection between our current media system and the declining state of American politics.[6]

Social trends show a public turning off to both politics and the press. In a sobering study released in 1990, and titled "The Age of Indifference," the Times Mirror Center for the People and the Press revealed that young Americans are less informed about current events than previous generations were. According to the report, the under-thirty generation "knows less, cares less and reads newspapers less than any generation in the past five decades." The sharp drop in newspaper readership was the survey's most dramatic revelation. Only 30 percent of Americans under thirty-five said they had "read a newspaper yesterday," compared with 67 percent of young people who answered the question affirmatively in a 1965 Gallup Poll. The study also revealed that young people were 20 percent less likely to say they followed important news stories. Moreover, this informational generation gap has widened drastically in recent years; surveys conducted in the 1940s, 1950s, and 1960s showed that young people were just as interested as their elders in major stories like the McCarthy hearings and the Vietnam War. But since the mid-seventies, the under-thirty group has been tuning out.[7] The result is a generation that votes less and is less critical of government and business. Interestingly, this tuning-out occurred just as the press was pushing for greater freedoms. Yet perhaps the increased emphasis on a fourth estate role of the press and the corresponding decline of public involvement in that press has contributed to the growing indifference toward and ignorance of current affairs.

Throughout American history, as discussed further in chapter 10, the periods of the most aggressive adversarial journalism have also been the periods of greatest public apathy toward the political process. When the press has ignored its social dialogue role and acted primarily as an aloof social critic and investigator, it has often alienated the public from both the press and politics. The muckraking journalism of the late nineteenth and early twentieth centuries provides one such example. Instead of inspiring the public to become politically involved, the muckrakers' ceaseless exposés of government corruption and social problems caused disillusionment and cynicism.[8] The press' harshly adversarial role eventually turned off large numbers of voters. Its unintended

message to the public was to be suspicious of the political process, to pull back from political commitment, and to stay home on
election day. Indeed, by definition, the fourth estate model seems
to breed a certain degree of political apathy. It asserts that the
health of a democracy depends on the ability of the press to act as
a watchdog on government, rather than on the public's involvement in the political and social dialogue process.

The increasing prevalence of negative journalism from a
watchdog-type press aggravates the problem of political apathy.
This brand of journalism further drills into an apathetic public all
the ills of society and government. It provides no outlet or opportunity for the public to reaffirm what is right and valuable. The
media's obsession with scandals, for instance, has produced widespread feelings of political cynicism and powerlessness. Indeed,
since the 1970s, the attack mode of American journalism has been
clearly evident. As Larry Sabato notes, journalists all too often
resemble gossip mongers more interested in scandal than substance who trivialize campaigns, scare away good candidates, and
turn off the voters. Indeed, the list is long: Geraldine Ferraro's
finances and Tom Eagleton's electroshocks; Ted Kennedy's
womanizing and Ed Muskie crying in New Hampshire; Gerald
Ford on Poland, Gary Hart sailing with Donna Rice, and the late
Wilbur Mills swimming with Fanne Foxe; Dan Quayle's academic record and Douglas Ginsburg's drug record; John Tower's
drinking, Chuck Robb's social liaisons, John Sununu's travel
schedule, and Bill Clinton's entire personal history. Sabato argues
that since the mid-1970s journalism has been driven by "junk-
yard dogs," lusting for fame and fortune and eager to tear their
victims to shreds. It is a natural outgrowth of an adversarial,
watchdog press.[9]

This adversarial stance has carried over to the press' relations
with the public. Indeed, perhaps the most tragic example is one of
a reporter sticking a camera and mike into a mother's face and
asking her how she feels about the shooting of her child, still lying
in a drawer in some hospital morgue. These images reflect a press
that has seemingly turned against the public it is supposed to
serve. It also appears that an adversarial press has turned from
investigating government and has instead focused on the public in

the search for real-life drama. The spectacle of the televised trials of Marlon Brando's son and the Menendez brothers, for example, seems to reflect this phenomenon, along with the real-life focus of popular television-tabloid shows like "A Current Affair" and "Trial Watch." Finally, the reluctant admission by Arthur Ashe in April 1992 that he had AIDS—an admission forced by *USA Today*—provided yet another indication that the media has turned against the public in its search for exposure and sensationalism.

Over the last several decades, a fourth-estate–type press has discouraged public involvement in the kind of dialogue on political and social issues that might in the future be possible through the new media technologies, and which a democracy desperately needs. In its coverage of political events and issues, for instance, the mass media has increasingly relied on a select group of so-called experts and commentators. These "sound-bite superstars" come from an elite Washington community of academics, politicos, journalists, lawyers, lobbyists, strategists, and authors who by themselves conduct most of the political dialogue in the press and attempt to present the public's views on public issues. These "experts" often represent a very narrow section of the population, and they crowd out participation by a broader section of the public. This use of experts also makes the inclusion of minority views and candidates, as well as newcomers to the political scene, more difficult. The result creates another gap between the media and the electorate and increases the tendency to rely on sound bites, oversimplify the issues, and filter out complications.[10]

The insider approach is further reinforced by the growing media practice of elevating the press into news subjects as well as news reporters. The modern media has further alienated its audience by turning its news coverage from the world of the public to the world of itself—the media. Increasingly, for instance, the media reports on politics by examining its own coverage of politics. For weeks after the publication of the Gary Hart scandal, the media dwelled on its role in that scandal, virtually ignoring the wider impact on the presidential campaign and on Gary Hart himself. In the 1992 campaign, news programs like "Nightline" continued to analyze the media's portrayal of character issues, just as they had four years before. Indeed, journalists seem obsessed with stories about themselves, even if the public has little interest in those stories.

Unquestionably, the power and practices of the news media over the last several decades have become a substantial part of the news. Plagiarism and other ethical violations in the newsroom have been well publicized, including stories about a *Wall Street Journal* reporter who accepted from Donald Trump three thousand-dollar tickets to a prizefight; a *Washington Post* reporter fired for lifting language from a *Miami Herald* story; a *New York Times* reporter suspended for taking information from a *Boston Globe* story about, of all things, a college dean reprimanded for plagiarism. In a way, the press has brought these troubles on itself. In becoming a concentrated and monopolized "fourth estate," the press had implicitly assured the public that its power and professionalism would provide accurate and objective reporting. Consequently, with so little debate and so few differences existing in the press, the public tends to expect the truth from every literal statement made by the press. The truth then comes not from a marketplace of ideas but from a monopolistic and homogeneous "all-knowing press." As a result, the press has more responsibility to get everything it says right.

The fourth estate view has furnished an incomplete and one-sided view of the press, emphasizing only the investigative and adversarial roles of the press. Its major fault, especially in light of the possibilities offered by the new media technologies, lies in its failure to recognize the vital press role of providing a forum for social dialogue. While the fourth estate model arose from the needs and demands of the established press of the 1970s, it seems ill equipped to protect an emerging press that does not rely solely on journalists and that involves greater public participation in the communication process.[11]

During the First Amendment activism of the 1960s and 1970s, press clause freedoms became a kind of "interest-group" right. Through the judicial decisions of that era, the majority of press freedoms focused almost exclusively on a specific group—journalists; indeed, the First Amendment seemed applicable only to journalists and their activities. Thus, the First Amendment came to be perceived as protecting a special privileged group, with no relevance or applicability to the general public.

The interest-group approach of the fourth estate model rose in prominence at the same time that interest-group politics came to dominate the political process. In interest-group politics, the group looks skeptically on society and strives to cement its interests into rights that are immune from political negotiation. Not only does the group not share in a common interest or purpose with society, it attempts to insulate itself from society.

Interest-group politics, however, has come under great attack.[12] The widespread perception of Walter Mondale as a pawn of interest groups, for instance, demonstrated the public antipathy toward such politics and contributed to Mondale's defeat in the 1984 presidential election. This backlash against such politics and the perceived prevalence of special interest-group rights has also spilled over to the press; journalists also have been perceived as having successfully created special privileges for themselves, casting themselves as victims of social intolerance, too readily resorting to the courts to obtain special treatment, and being generally unconcerned with the public's interest and the common good. Consequently, this interest-group image of journalists has somewhat antagonized the public and thereby created pressures for changes in the First Amendment press doctrines.

In reaction to these interest-group rights, and in an effort to curb abuses by journalists, the public has moved to expand its freedom to influence the images and information communicated by the media.[13] This reaction seems to be reflected in a series of Supreme Court decisions in the early 1990s that seem to curb the abuses of a fourth estate press and make it more accountable to its news sources and subjects. In *Cohen v. Cowles Media Co.*, the Court in a slim five-to-four majority held that the First Amendment does not insulate the press from liability for a broken promise of confidentiality to an informant. In *Masson v. The New Yorker Magazine*, 111 S.Ct. 2419 (1991), a libel action based on allegedly fabricated quotations attributed to the plaintiff, the Supreme Court ruled that a deliberate alteration of quotes could provide the basis for a libel action and were not protected by the press' constitutional libel privilege. Earlier, in *Milkovich v. Lorain Journal Co.*, 110 S. Ct. 2965 (1990), the Court found that certain expressions of opinion could be subject to a libel action and concluded that a newspaper columnist's statements implied that the plaintiff had perjured himself in judicial proceedings and hence did not qualify as constitutionally protected opinion. Under the Court's holding, statements of opinion that can reasonably be interpreted as stating or implying false assertions of fact may legitimately form the basis of a defamation action. The decisions in *Cohen, Masson,* and *Milkovich* may reflect a judicial desire to move away from a journalist model of the press and toward a more public-oriented model. They may also reflect an intent to equalize somewhat the public's position in respect to the media, to help prevent the public from being dominatetd by a monopolized mass media perceived as irresponsible and predatory. These cases may further indicate a certain desire to end the perceived monopolization of the First Amendment by journalists. As the new interactive media promises to involve a wider public, however, this desire may be realized as First Amendment press freedoms expand to cover the new technologies.

Yet for this goal to be realized, changes in First Amendment press doctrines must occur. A new constitutional model of the press is needed since the new technologies do not squarely fall within the fourth estate view of the press. Moreover, when articulated in theh 1970s, the fourth estate model was based perhaps more upon reactions to recent historical events where the press opposed an apparently secretive and corrupt government—for example, during Watergate and Vietnam—than upon an overall analysis of the historical workings of the press and the values expected of a free press in a democratic society. A more complete historical examination, however, reveals that the American press, for most of the last three centuries, has been more of an opinionated and participatory press than it has been a fourth-estate–type press. The following chapter further demonstrates that the historical and constitutional identity of the press is not adequately described by the fourth estate model. It also suggests the type of press that the First Amendment should protect during the upcoming period of media change

■ PART IV ■

Shaping New First Amendment
Doctrines by Defining the Press

Like all previous First Amendment press doctrines, the fourth
estate model reflects the press industry as it existed when the
model was enacted. Yet most disputes and controversies in
prior First Amendment adjudication have not required a definition of the press. Obviously, the press litigants in the past have
simply asserted their identity as the press, and the courts have
accepted that assertion.

The increasing number and diversity of future media organizations made possible by technological advances, however,
will soon change the old habit of defining as the press anyone
who claims to represent the press. With more and more diverse
parties claiming to represent "the press," the courts will have
to establish some defining test which transcends the self-given
labels of individual media-related entities, such as that used by
the courts in connection with the First Amendment religion
clause. Rather than accept without question the claims of each
person seeking exemption from some state law because of his
religious beliefs or of each religious group seeking tax-exempt
status, the courts apply various constitutional tests to determine
whether those religious beliefs or those religious organizations
meet the standards for First Amendment protection.

In seeking a constitutional definition of the press—one that
will direct the First Amendment in a future age of technological change—it is necessary to first examine the identity of the
press as it existed at the time of the drafting of the First Amendment. In striving to move the free press clause away from an
interest-group orientation, the values and purposes of a free
press must be clarified. In this way, a functional and more
timeless definition of the press can be reached.

8

The Historical Identity of the American Press

THE "PRESS" that is protected by the constitution has never been clearly defined by the courts, even though First Amendment cases have been adjudicated since the 1920s. Of course, during most of the twentieth century the press has been a fairly static industry. Newspapers have existed during the entire century, and broadcast television news departments arose around mid-century. Consequently, those two groups—print and broadcast television—have informally defined the constitutional press and have brought the vast majority of press cases to the courts.

However, because the press cases of the future will no longer involve only the neatly defined print and broadcast journalists, the need to define the press as it is protected by the First Amendment becomes all the more urgent. Engineers and technocrats have described the kind of press and communications system that will evolve over the next decade and have spoken of almost magical machines that will connect every home to almost every conceivable source of information. But this plethora of predictions does not in turn produce an understanding of the constitutional definition of the press of the future. Perhaps the starting point for such an understanding lies not in the future but in the past.

One way to define the constitutionally protected press is to examine the type of press with which the framers of the First Amendment were familiar when they extended constitutional protections to the press. Such a historical examination can transcend the narrow bounds of the specific media technologies existing at any one time. It can also help define the press on a broader and more comprehensive level than that afforded by the litigation process.

Presumably, the framers of the Constitution would have wanted to protect the type of press existing at the time they drafted the First Amendment. This kind of historical approach was suggested by the Commission on the Freedom of the Press when it speculated on the meaning of "freedom of the press" at the time of the Constitution by focusing on the actual workings of the colonial press. Leonard Levy likewise argues that "when the framers of the First Amendment provided that Congress shall not abridge the freedom of the press they could only have meant to protect the press with which they were familiar and as it operated at the time." He believes that the free press clause recognized and strove to perpetuate the kind of press industry that existed in the late eighteenth century.[1] Therefore, a historical examination of the eighteenth-century press provides valuable guidelines for broadly defining the type of press intended to be protected under the First Amendment.

The Interactive Press in Colonial America

Like the new media technologies of the late twentieth century, the press in the eighteenth century was highly interactive. During the colonial period, printers ordinarily edited and published their own newspapers, but they did not write most of the articles and essays. Instead, they solicited contributing pieces from outside authors and subscribers. The content of colonial newspapers closely mirrored the attitudes and desires of the community. Political discussion in the press was geared to the issues important to the local constituencies. Newspapers contained everything from advertisements to literary essays, political polemics, and news. Essentially, colonial newspapers were bulletin boards for their communities; they were both subject to and responsive to the wishes of colonial society.[2]

The pivotal role in gathering information and opinions was held not by the printer but by his contributors and information sources. Most editors envisioned their jobs as providing opportunities to express partisan views on social topics and public affairs. In this sense, the press served as an organ through which the literate public could, and very often did, voice their political and social opinions.[3]

Compared with the larger printing operations in England, even the most successful printing shops in the American colonies were modest enterprises. The threat of competition and of an exodus of subscribers continually prevailed. More than half of the 2,120 newspapers established between 1690 and 1820 expired before they were two years old, and only 34 percent lasted a generation.[4]

The Opinion Role of the Press

With the escalation of the conflict with England in the latter half of the eighteenth century, printers in the colonies eventually gave up their attempt to be impartial in their political essays and instead began to be quite opinionated. More than twice as many chose the patriot side as did the Tory side. During the prolonged crisis of the revolutionary period, printers began to act in ways that promoted a politics expressive of conflict and dissent. This practice contrasted with that of the earlier colonial period, when impartiality was followed more closely and the colonial newspapers served primarily as indiscriminate forums for public debate.[5]

Public expectations of the role of American printers were being reshaped by the revolutionary conflict. Through the journalistic marketplace, the colonists were registering their embrace of patriot views and rejection of the Tory position. Many patriot printers reacted to the heightened political mood of the public by expressing strong political views.[6] Thus, the political and opinionated journalism of the revolutionary period was market-driven, and the printers were responding to the views and demands of the community they served. As Benjamin Franklin remarked, "the business of printing has chiefly to do with men's opinions."[7]

Very gradually there arose from the revolutionary experience a revised understanding of the role of an American printer. Responding to a new belief that sharply antagonistic opinions might properly be articulated in the public forum, printers in America began to discard their previously proclaimed impartiality and to behave aggressively and unapologetically as partisans. Consequently, the increasingly opinionated newspapers reflected the intense ideological content of revolutionary politics. At the same time, the principle of freedom of the press underwent a significant change. It now justified the political activism of the patriot press, and, despite the claims of the pro-British printers, freedom of the press no longer required editorial impartiality.[8]

During the colonial and postrevolutionary periods, the press served as a vehicle for espousing the interests of one group against those of another—colonists against Royal governors, revolutionists against Tories, and generally outsiders against insiders in government. Indeed, almost every newspaper served as a channel for public debate and became a free forum for the discussion of politics. No one newspaper could represent all or nearly all of the conflicting viewpoints regarding public issues. Presumably, together, all of the newspapers would do so. If they did not, the person whose opinions were not represented could start another newspaper.[9]

The British passage and enforcement of the Stamp Act and later the Townshend Acts catalyzed the American press as forums for political debate. The campaign against the Stamp Act greatly increased the opinion role of newspapers. No longer "mere transmitters of information, they had become engines of opinion." Indeed, in the period preceding the revolution, several newspapers served strictly as journals of opinion and did not even bother to print hard news.[10]

The newspapers carried forward the role they had played in the Stamp Act crisis to protest against the Townshend Acts. Even more so than the Stamp Act, the Townshend Acts sparked an intense battle of opinion between the patriot press and the progovernment press.

During the controversy surrounding the Stamp Act and Townshend Acts, printers were greatly swayed by the opinions of their readers. The more radical the readers, the bolder the printers. The content of colonial newspapers closely mirrored the particular issues which were important to the local constituencies, so the press in effect became intertwined with local partisan battles, and newspapers often started up just as political issues rose in importance. The newspaper campaign against the Townshend Act, for example, reflected and expressed the popular opposition to those measures.[11] And throughout the journalistic debate on the Tea

Act, the content of the newspapers leaned more toward opinions, essays, and propaganda than toward objective news. Indeed, by the time of the outbreak of hostilities in 1775, almost every newspaper in the colonies could be clearly identified as either patriot or Tory. Subsequently, in the journalistic battle during the Revolutionary War, the debate in the press continued to be intensely opinionated and partisan.[12]

Long after independence, newspapers continued to express political opinion, and partisan journalism became a well-established feature of American politics. As the Reverend Samuel Miller observed at the start of the nineteenth century, the newspapers of America were "immense, moral and political engines" that advanced opinions as well as reported occurrences.[13] By 1800, political opinion had become the staple of American journalism.

The Competitive Colonial Printing Industry

The newspaper industry that faced the framers of the First Amendment in 1791 was comprised of many small-scale enterprises. Any individual wishing to enter into the pamphlet, book, and newspaper publishing industry could readily do so. Communications dominated by significant scale economies were unknown by the framers of the First Amendment. In their experience, "economic competition was consistent with the political function of the press because of the small-scale technology of printing and the rapid rate of entry in the industry in the decade preceding 1791."[14] Indeed, the availability of inexpensive printing presses, along with the political ferment of the time, fueled the growth of the penny press in the nineteenth century, which were often started not by industrialists but by skilled workers.

During the revolutionary period, the low barriers to entry into the newspaper business produced many new ventures. The decade of the 1780s witnessed extraordinary growth in the number of newspapers. In all, 450 newspapers were started in the period from 1783 to 1801.[15] Competition between presses was stiff. All of the larger settlements had competing print shops after about 1730. As the conflict with Great Britain worsened, printers needed to be especially in tune with the political wishes and opinions of their readers; therefore, they maintained a keen awareness of who their readers were and whether they harbored loyalist or patriotic tendencies. In short, presses were subordinate to the wishes of society as long as society was not completely disinterested.

Characterized by many publications reflecting highly partisan viewpoints, the early American press constituted a true marketplace of ideas in which there was relatively easy access to the channels of communication. Speech and publishing in 1791 emanated from relatively fragmented sources rather than from integrated, highly organized media forms.

The Political Role of the Press in Revolutionary America

Throughout the revolutionary crisis, patriots generally agreed that without a free press they could never have hoped to gain independence.[16] Even by the 1740s the press had become an indispensable part of politics, being used both for campaigning purposes and as a means of pressuring those already in office to adopt a particular course of action. For example, in 1754 seventeen pamphlets appeared in Boston to protest a liquor excise bill under consideration by the Massachusetts legislature, and this outburst resulted in the legislature's rejection of the bill.[17]

To colonial Americans the press offered a remedy for their most chronic ailment—disunity.[18] Recognition of this role and purpose of a free press may also be found in the *Address to the Inhabitants of Quebec,* which was sent to Quebec in October 1775 by the First Continental Congress in order to garner the Canadians' support in the fight against British oppression. Designed to outline the rights for which they were fighting, the Continental Congress articulated the importance of freedom of the press:

> The last right we shall mention, regards freedom of the press. The importance of this consists, besides the advancement of truth, science, morality, and arts in general, in its diffusion of liberal sentiments on the administration of government, its ready communication of thoughts between subjects, and its consequential promo-

tion of union among them, whereby oppressive officers are shamed or intimidated, into more honorable and just modes of conducting their affairs.[19]

Throughout the revolutionary period, the press consistently reflected the political life and interests of the nation. At times, it both molded public opinion and mirrored it. However, seldom has the press accomplished both functions so completely as in the years immediately following the ratification of the federal Constitution. The dispute with Britain had led many Americans to seriously examine the nature of government itself, and this dialogue aired in the newspapers and continued in the 1790s when the development of political parties led to the creation of a partisan press. Both Republicans and Federalists participated in forming party presses, and, of the more than 350 newspapers published in 1810, all but approximately fifty had a political affiliation.[20]

An important change in the character of the press in the period from 1783 to 1791 occurred as newspapers increasingly became the appointed voices of political parties. As partisan activity grew in the new nation, the public came to recognize an additional reason for the existence of newspapers—the dissemination of partisan ideas. Following the war, newspapers were increasingly started as arms of political parties and began acting as their semiofficial vehicles. This gave a new dimension to American journalism and resulted in the emergence of the newspaper editor, who assumed more responsibility for choosing and coordinating the viewpoints expressed in their newspapers. Yet even though newspapers became increasingly partisan, they still served as forums for public debate.[21]

It was quickly recognized that the new democratic nation needed a free press as a "bulletin board" of public opinion. The Republicans valued a free press because of their belief that public opinion was more than a cyclical phenomenon registering itself every two years at the polls; it was in a continuous process of formulation and could be conveyed simultaneously through the press. According to Republicans, newspapers served as the best channel for conveying advice to those in power and for releasing the pent-up emotions of those out of power. Whether applauded or depreciated, in reality the press was the conduit between each party's leaders and the public.[22]

The opinion power of the press was well recognized at the time. Indeed, by the end of the war, public opinion had become the basis of American democratic development. The impact of the press during the revolutionary period had not only instilled a newspaper-reading habit in the American public, but also firmly established the opinion-making function of the press and thereby contributed substantially to the democratization of American politics. Newspapers also were an important tool for the political leadership. For if, as Edmund Morgan argues, the American Revolution was an intellectual movement in which politics replaced religion as the chief concern of the colonial leadership, newspapers became the equivalent of secular Bibles.[23]

According to Thomas Leonard, the early press, by creating a social forum for political dialogue, motivated Americans to pay attention to their government, to welcome public discourse, and to vote. To Leonard, the achievement of democratic participation was left to the press. He argues that the press provided the vernacular for the discussion of issues, made political debate legitimate, and served as the chief forum for public controversy. In essence, the development of the American press led to the rise of democratic political participation.[24]

Conclusion

The press during the revolutionary and constitutional periods was characterized by competitive, small-scale printers. They published their newspapers without any editors or reporters and left the role of news gathering up to their readers. Essentially, printers acted like a sort of community bulletin board through which their readers could communicate. The eighteenth-century press consequently served primarily as a forum for community communication and political debate.

The drafters of the First Amendment realized that communication through the newspapers had been a necessary requisite for political action. The accessible and participatory press had helped create a unified movement for independence and a national political system. And the realization of the press' political role greatly inspired the drafting of the First Amendment press clause.

In examining the historical roots of the American press, the divergence of the contemporary press from these roots becomes apparent. Large-scale concentrated media corporations have replaced the independent printer. Most towns and cities have only one newspaper, many of which are chain-owned. Local responsiveness has also diminished, since chain-owned newspapers and television stations often reflect more the dictates of the corporate chain than a "bulletin board" of the community. Ironically, the concentration that has occurred in the press industry has raised fears that four centuries of press struggles to break the licensing bonds of governments has only resulted in a new variety of restraints and a new kind of censor in the form of monopolistic corporations.

News gathering and reporting roles have also changed. Professional journalists now investigate and write the stories that appear in the press, and even the shrinking editorial pages are devoted to professional columnists. In short, the modern press is one in which the input has drastically changed from the subscribing public to the professional journalists. It has consequently become less a forum for public participation in the communication process than one devoted to a class of professional journalists. As a result, the public has been increasingly pushed away from the press and from social dialogue.

Unlike the eighteenth-century press, in which its readers actively participated, the public today no longer plays a vital or even active role in the media. It has become simply a passive consumer of the news and advertising. The contemporary press often treats news and information as a commodity, as something to be supplied to a consuming public, whereas the eighteenth-century press treated the content of its newspapers as the expressions of a communicating public. The colonial press did not stand apart from its subscribers in an objective, aloof role but very much expressed the pulse of local public opinion.

The modern media has blurred our historical memory of the American press. Indeed, with the growth and diversity of the American population and with the increasing complexity and economic costs of the modern media enterprises, it has been assumed that a participatory press similar to the eighteenth-century press is no longer possible. Yet perhaps the coming technological innovations will enable America to once again experience an activist and participatory press—one which energizes the political process instead of denigrating it. But most fundamentally, in an age of a changing and expanding press, the historical experience and identity of the American press provides an invaluable guide for shaping the press and the First Amendment doctrines of the future.

9

The Independent Nature of the First Amendment Press Clause

Introduction

DEFINING THE "PRESS" as it is protected under the First Amendment requires that a distinction be made between the speech clause and the press clause of the First Amendment. In comparison with the speech clause, the press clause has often seemed like a little brother—always in the shadow of the speech clause and often without a separate identity. Indeed, many constitutional scholars have argued that no difference exists between the two clauses and that the press clause simply protects the speech of those in the press business. Moreover, the Supreme Court has never ruled that the two clauses are distinct and, if they are, how they differ. Not until the press cases of the 1970s— which dealt with news-gathering rights—was the Court even presented with the question of whether the press clause protects something different from that protected by the speech clause. In these cases, the Court was not concerned with defining the press, but with determining what journalistic activities might receive constitutional protection.

The first influential effort to distinguish the speech and press clauses occurred with the publication of Justice Potter Stewart's "Or of the Press." In that article, Justice Stewart argued that if the press clause protected nothing more than what was protected under the speech clause, it would be a constitutional redundancy and would have been unnecessary to the text of the First Amendment.[1] Despite his arguments, however, the rest of the Court has never embraced a theory outlining the distinctions between the two clauses.

For most of the twentieth century, the First Amendment focus has been on the speech clause. In the First Amendment decisions of the World War I era, the emphasis was on defining the limits of permissible speech, especially when the government attempted to restrict speech that conflicted with mainstream social and political institutions and beliefs. These same questions returned in the speech cases of the 1950s and 1960s, when constitutional questions over the regulation of speech advocating radical ideas and communist beliefs continued to occupy the courts' First Amendment attentions.

Throughout the 1960s and 1970s, a period of great social turmoil and change, the limits of permissible speech were continually challenged:

- Could a person wear in public a jacket that carried an offensive statement like "Fuck the Draft"?
- Did the burning of a draft card constitute protected speech or impermissible conduct?
- Were state antisedition laws aimed at Communist advocacy unconstitutional?
- Did political demonstrators convicted for disorderly conduct have their speech freedoms violated?
- Could a private shopping center prohibit the distribution of handbills on its property?
- Did certain speech qualify as obscenity and hence fall outside constitutional protection?[2]

Even cases directly involving the media, such as *New York Times v. U.S.* (the Pentagon Papers case), turned on free speech issues like prior restraint. Thus, during the last First Amendment revolution, the courts largely dealt with questions concerning the limits on free expression and the extent of free speech rights. Consequently, in the American constitutional development, speech has been defined in detail.

On the most fundamental level, the courts have defined speech as an expression, rather than as conduct. Of course, the expression may take many forms, such as written, vocal, or artistic. It may also be expressed in language or may be expressed symbolically. After this fundamental inquiry is made, the constitutional protection of speech depends on its further definition or categorization. For instance, if speech is defined as "commercial speech," it receives less protection. If certain speech is found to be obscene or to constitute "fighting words," it loses its constitutional privileges. Dissident political speech can only be restricted if it advocates the use of force or other illegal action and is calculated to incite imminent lawless action.

This detailed judicial definition of speech has led the courts to develop comprehensive doctrines for its protection. Even a conservative Court recently upheld speech freedoms in its decision to overturn a flag desecration statute.[3] This same degree of judicial development and maturity, however, does not exist for the press clause. Yet prior to articulating a separate definition of "the press," as it appears in the First Amendment, the question must be answered about whether the two clauses—speech and press—are separate and distinct.

The Differences Between the Speech and Press Clauses

Protection of Different Values

In constructing a First Amendment theory of the press clause, an initial inquiry must aim at distinguishing between the speech and press clauses. The differences between the values and functions of free speech and a free press will in turn suggest the different protections and functions of the two clauses.

Much of the current debate over the press clause revolves around whether the speech and press clauses protect different freedoms. This debate was fueled by Justice Potter Stewart, when he suggested that there may be distinctive functions and features of "the press" that warrant a constitutional protection separate from that granted under the speech clause.[4]

Any difference between the speech and press clauses depends on the separate values or functions served by free speech and a free press in a democratic society. Currently, however, freedom of press is determined by the particular medium, rather than by the function and values of a free press. For instance, the government regulates broadcasting in certain ways because of the medium by which it is circulated, even though in function it probably has supplanted print as the primary source of news for many Americans and even though technology may have eliminated many of the original differences between print and broadcast media.

Therefore, defining the press as it is protected under the First Amendment initially requires an examination of the broad values with which the press clause is concerned. The next step will then be to determine how these values differ from those addressed by the speech clause.

The Attainment of Truth

The pursuit of truth as a value of free expression was firmly recognized in political thought for more than a century preceding the adoption of the First Amendment. John Milton, for instance, wrote in protest of the English system of licensing that truth is best tested and falsehood best suppressed when they compete against each other in the open marketplace of ideas. Later, the writings of John Stuart Mill strengthened the marketplace theory, and his essay *On Liberty* influenced the development of basic First Amendment beliefs. Mill advocated uninhibited expression as the best means for testing the truth of opinions, as well as for reinvigorating worthwhile beliefs. Significantly, he did not advocate free expression for any intrinsic value; he instead defended it as the best means of achieving a more fundamental goal—the spread of truth.[5]

American proponents of free expression at the time of the ratification of the Bill of Rights similarly believed that the value of uninhibited expression lay in the discovery of truth. Eighteenth-century defenders of a free press relied upon the concept of a ''marketplace of ideas'' and the ''belief that competing voices produce superior conclusions.'' The Continental Congress expressed this conviction throughout the almost two-decade span preceding the adoption of the First Amendment. In its address to the people of Quebec, for instance, the congress advocated freedom of the press on the grounds that it promoted truth.[6]

Twentieth-century theorists have continued to articulate the truth value of free expression. Zechariah Chafee found that ''one of the most important purposes of society and government is the discovery and spread of truth on subjects of general concern, [and that] this is possible only through absolutely unlimited discussion." Alexander Meiklejohn likewise argued that the framers enacted the constitutional protection of speech and press to ensure the dissemination of the kind of political truth required for reasoned self-government.[7]

The truth value underlying the First Amendment initially found its expression in constitutional law through the marketplace metaphor employed by Justice Oliver Wendell Holmes:

> But when men have realized that time has upset many fighting faiths, they may come to believe even more than they believe the very foundations of their own conduct that the ultimate good desire is better reached by free trade in ideas—that the best test of truth is the power of thought to get itself accepted in the competition of the market and that truth is the only ground upon which their wishes safely can be carried out.[8]

In *Whitney v. California,* 274 U.S. 357, 375 (1927) (Brandeis, J., concurring), Justice Louis Brandeis similarly stated that the First Amendment carries the assumption that free expression is indispensable to the "discovery and spread of political truth" and that the "greatest menace to people is an inert people." The marketplace metaphor again reappeared in *Associated Press v. United States,* 326 U.S. 1, 20 (1945), where the Supreme Court stated that the purpose of freedom of speech and press is to assure "the widest possible dissemination of information from diverse and antagonistic sources."[9]

The Promotion of a Democratic Government

One of the First Amendment's primary purposes is to support the democratic process. During the constitutional debates in the late eighteenth century, the focus of discussion was on the political role of the press and its relation to self-government. Under James Madison's conception of the First Amendment, a free press was "created less specifically to guarantee individual expression than to evoke the public debate that creates a vigorous society."[10]

The Supreme Court has also recognized this purpose as a primary function of free expression. The Court, for instance, found that the First Amendment "forbids the state from interfering with the communicative processes through which its citizens exercise and prepare to exercise their rights of self-govern-ment.''[11] This view of the First Amendment recognizes that a society cannot intelligently make decisions required of a self-governing people unless all possible views are expressed. It also puts at the core of the First Amendment the relationship between freedom of the press and the political process.

A free press promotes the rational and well-reasoned opera-tion of government. According to Alexander Meiklejohn, a cen-tral purpose of the First Amendment, if not its exclusive purpose, is to sustain the process of representative self-government. Meik-lejohn views the self-government rationale as a function distinct from and superior to the truth function:

> The First Amendment is not, primarily, a device for the winning of new truth, though that is very important. It is a device for the sharing of whatever truth has been won. Its purpose is to give to every voting member of the body politic the fullest possible participation in the understanding of those problems with which the citizens of a self-governing society must deal.[12]

This self-government value, sometimes called the democratic di-alogue function, is especially applicable to the press. Communi-cation through the press contributes more significantly to the democratic dialogue than does speech through other channels.[13]

Not only does a free press aid in the rational functioning of self-government, it also promotes citizen participation in govern-ment and the formation of political majorities, which are needed in a democracy. The political process begins not at the ballot box, but at the point where groups begin identifying political issues and communicating together. Without a free and accessible press, political groups could not even begin communicating their posi-tions and identities with the rest of society.[14] Political majorities cannot be formed, and majority decisions cannot be made, with-out free and open dissemination of ideas. The Constitution's main function is to allow groups to participate in forming coalitions so as to engage in the democratic process.[15] Thus, democratic gov-ernment requires not only free and well-informed debate on the issues, but also a forum in which citizens can participate in the public discussion of issues which then leads to the formation of factions and groups. Therefore, separate from the function of "advancing knowledge and discovering truth," a free press provides for participation by all members of society in political decision making.[16]

The press' participatory value also carries beyond the political realm, extending to the public's ability to build and maintain a democratic society in all its forms, including its religious, cultural, and intellectual sides. Indeed, a close connection exists between an open and freely competitive press and the promotion of democratic pluralism.[17]

The Promotion of Democratic Society

Social bonds between individuals require social communication. Apart from its relation to the workings of representative government, free and open communication is essential for the formation and maintenance of a democratic society, which, in turn, is a prerequisite for self-government. The First Amendment preserves these social and political foundations since the press provides the primary forum for the kind of open and participatory communication needed for democratic society building. According to David Schuman, "the Framers conceived the First Amendment to facilitate a broadly based and inclusive public discourse."[18]

Freedom to communicate gives individuals the ability to create a common, social world. Communication not only articulates social interests but, in fact, forms and develops them. As Hannah Arendt has noted, a "life without speech ceases to be a human life . . . communication affirms our reality." Without speech as a mode of unity, neither the reality of one's self nor of the surrounding world can be known. Communication, therefore, is essential for social interaction and unity. Indeed, the rise of the modern nation-state and the spirit of nationalism often occurs under the banner of improved communications.[19]

Open communication provides the social cohesiveness necessary for a democratic social structure to survive. Government by itself cannot produce the social cohesion necessary to stabilize the political branch of society. Freedom of communication, therefore, constitutes a precondition of all forms of democratic political organizations.[20] It gives individuals the power to create a common world—a public realm—which is necessary for the democratic organization of society.

A constitutional theory of a free press should recognize the role played by a communications system in building a democratic culture and society. Although many First Amendment scholars have addressed the connection between the First Amendment and the maintenance of democratic government, fewer have examined the more complex but vital web of relationships between free expression, the nature of culture and society, and the health of democratic government. A number of twentieth-century writers, beginning with John Dewey, have concluded that the cultural conditions for democracy must exist before democratic government can thrive. Dewey theorized that political freedom could not be maintained without an existing culture of freedom. Thus, while democratic government arises out of democratic society and culture, free expression and open channels of social communication constitute an important ingredient of a democratic culture. Democracy is a "process of persuasion through which citizens seek to create and maintain a good life in common."[21]

According to Dewey, the problem of freedom and of democratic institutions "is tied up with the question of what kind of culture exists, with the necessity of free culture for free political institutions" (p. 13). He believed that the social channels of communication are a fundamental element in determining the nature of society and its resulting political institutions. Dewey denied that democratic institutions automatically maintain themselves, or that they could be created simply by a constitution. The framers, according to Dewey, understood these strong cultural influences on political institutions. Under Dewey's theories, free and open expression is one of those essential conditions for creating the kind of culture that can maintain a democratic political order. And an independent press is an essential ingredient for free and open social communication.[22]

The exchange of ideas through a free press allows society to become aware of the cultural conditions needed for a workable and responsive democratic system of government. More than a formal political mechanism, democracy encompasses the way people regulate their relationships with others and with the state. A free press, by facilitating social interchange, makes such relationships possible and constructive.

Freedom of expression leads to a more adaptable and stable

community. The absence of communication opportunities, on the other hand, promotes inflexibility and prevents society from adjusting to changing circumstances and from developing new ideas. Furthermore, the process of open discussion through the press promotes greater cohesion in society because individuals are more ready to accept decisions that go against them if they have an opportunity to communicate their opinions.[23]

Justice Louis Brandeis, in his seminal opinion in *Whitney v. California,* 274 U.S. 357, 375 1927, stressed this relationship between public order and free expression. For Brandeis, the First Amendment expresses the belief that ''the path of safety lies in the opportunity to discuss freely supposed grievances and proposed remedies'' (375). It has been suggested that the contemporary threat to Brandeis's ''path of safety'' lies in the lack of opportunity for the disadvantaged and the dissatisfied of our society to discuss supposed grievances effectively.[24] Therefore, a further value of the safety valve function lies in the opportunity that freedom of speech gives to persons in power to learn about and respond to grievances before citizens become irretrievably alienated.

The Watchdog Value of the Press

A free press can alert the public to abuses and incidents of corruption in government. Under this ''watchdog'' role, the press acts as an agent of the public and serves as an additional check on the three official branches. The watchdog value of the press was articulated by Vincent Blasi and formed the focus of the fourth estate model of the press described in chapter 6.

The Separate Values Protected by the Speech and Press Clauses

Within the broad framework of the values of a system of free expression outlined above, there are different values and functions protected by the press and speech clauses that demand separate constitutional protections. While the speech clause protects individuals in their act of speaking, the press clause protects the dissemination of those views and assures an open forum for communication in society and for democratic political dialogue. The press clause does not merely protect individuals in the act of printing or broadcasting their ideas—the speech clause adequately serves that purpose. In effect, the distinction is one between free speech and the conditions necessary for its expression. Thus, the free press clause protects the maintenance of conditions conducive to the democratic dialogue.

Individualistic and Societal Values

Individual free expression, protected by the free speech clause, preserves the individual's dignity and autonomy.[25] This self-fulfillment function of speech finds no counterpart in relation to the press, especially given the corporate makeup of the media. While the free speech clause rests upon the view that society must respect individual autonomy as an end in itself, the press clause is directed more to the dissemination of individual speech in society and to the nature of the institutions which disseminate that speech.[26]

The speech clause is fundamentally concerned with individualistic values—the freedom of the individual to express his or her opinions free of social control. The press clause, on the other hand, is concerned primarily with social and political values. Unlike the speech clause, the press clause protects values that relate to the functioning of the political process and democratic society.

Justice Lewis Powell's opinions illustrate this distinction between the individual and the social values underlying the two clauses. In his dissent in *Saxbe v. Washington Post Company,* 417 U.S. 817 (1974), and his opinion in *First National Bank v. Bellotti,* 435 U.S. 765 (1978), Justice Powell espoused a societal function of the First Amendment, which focused on preserving an open system of public affairs discussion. Zechariah Chafee had likewise envisioned the First Amendment guarantees of freedom of speech and press as protecting two kinds of interests: those of individuals to express their opinions, and those of society's attainment of truth.[27] Thus, the individualistic and societal values of the First Amendment coincide with the speech and press clauses respectively, and the societal function relates to the maintenance of an open and competitive press industry that serves the needs of a democratic society.

Justice William Brennan's opinions also suggest that the First Amendment affords protection not only for communication itself, but for the conditions necessary for meaningful communication. In an October 1979 speech, Brennan identified two types of First Amendment protection: the speech model and the structural model. The speech model obviously refers to the speech protections given by the First Amendment. The structural model, however, can be likened to the press clause. Under Brennan's structural model, the "First Amendment protects the structure of communications necessary for the existence of democracy. This . . . describes the role of the press in our society. It focuses on the relationship of the press to the communicative functions required by our democratic beliefs." Brennan's two-part view of the First Amendment distinguished the press clause, which protects the social channels of democratic communication, from the speech clause, which covers the specific utterances of individuals.[28]

The societal function found in the press clause follows from the First Amendment's concern with democratic processes:

> No aspect of that Constitutional guaranty of the First Amendment is more rightly treasured than its protection of the ability of our people through free and open debate to consider and resolve their own destiny . . . the First Amendment is one of the vital bulwarks of our national commitment to intelligent self-government.

Rather than protecting certain specific individual rights or activities, the press clause serves as a broader protection of the social communicative process that leads to self-government.[29]

The speech clause of the First Amendment, though primarily concerned with preserving individual liberty, also enhances the democratic process. However, the value to democratic government does not by itself justify the free speech clause. That clause is based upon a respect for individual rights and dignity. The free press clause, on the other hand, more directly focuses on the public interest in promoting democratic society and government. Indeed, the interests of democracy provide the ultimate justification for press rights.[30] The press clause therefore aims more at providing a forum or marketplace for individual speech than in protecting the act of speaking and the content of the particular speech, which is protected by the speech clause.

The societal interpretation of the press clause essentially focuses on a literal view of the First Amendment language. The speech clause protects the act of speaking and extends to those who are capable of speaking. But the First Amendment also protects "the press," which preserves a communications forum made up of competitive and independent press entities, facilitating the discussion of public affairs. Insofar as the press discharges this societal function, it is entitled to First Amendment protection.[31]

The Analogy to the Establishment of Religion Clause

The speech and press clauses can be compared to the religious exercise and establishment clauses of the First Amendment. The speech clause, like the free religious exercise clause, protects the individual's private sphere of freedom. Conversely, the press clause, like the religious establishment clause, protects the public interest in a particular structure of important nongovernmental institutions in society. While the religious establishment clause governs the relationship between religion and government, the press clause governs the relationship between social communication forums and the political process.

First Amendment scholars have likewise suggested that the religious establishment of the religion clause in the First Amendment provides a helpful analogy to use in understanding the press clause. They recognize that both the religious establishment clause and the press clause protect the independence and integrity of vital nongovernmental centers of expression and power. Thus, by analogy, we can interpret some First Amendment clauses (free religious exercise and free speech) as focused on individual liberty and others (the religious establishment and press clauses) as focused on principles that apply to the relation between government and specific institutions existing in society.[32]

A Structural Provision

The free speech clause protects individuals in the act of speaking and communicating. Its protection adapts to the individual and, as such, constitutes an individual right or liberty. The press clause, on the other hand, does not focus strictly on individual rights and liberties, but must be seen as a broader protection—a structural provision of the Constitution. This structural aspect of the press clause arises from its attachment to the press as an industry and social communication forum rather than to specific individual activities.

Justice Potter Stewart has recognized the structural feature of the press clause and has advocated this view in First Amendment adjudication:

> Most of the other provisions in the Bill of Rights protects specific liberties or specific rights of individuals . . . in contrast, the free press clause extends protection to an institution. The publishing business is, in short, the only organized business that is given explicit constitutional protection.[33]

In *Richmond Newspapers, Inc. v. Virginia,* 448 U.S. (1980) at 587, Justice William Brennan also stated that ''the First Amendment embodies more than a commitment to free expression and communicative interchange for their own sakes: it has a structural role to play in securing and fostering our republican system of self-government.''

Ithiel de Sola Pool similarly adopted a structural view and argues for an open and competitive press. He advocated government regulation over the media only to the extent that a particular media actually is monopolized. By urging government regulation only when a monopoly exists, Pool argued that communication mediums should be decentralized, dispersed, and competitive. Thus, Pool took a structural approach and accords constitutional protection only to an open and competitive press. A press characterized by monopoly conditions, on the other hand, does not receive protection and, as Pool argued, should be subject to governmental regulation.[34]

A structural view of the press clause means that the First Amendment only protects a certain kind of press industry. The model of such a protected industry is found in the eighteenth-century press—a competitive, participatory press industry that offers easy entry and is free of government-created monopolies. This structural view combines with a description of the values served by a free press to define ''the press'' as it appears in the text of the First Amendment. Therefore, the press clause addresses the type of communication system needed to facilitate the search for social truth, to provide for expression of diverse opinions, to encourage widespread social participation in the communicative and political process, and to serve as a watchdog on government.

The actual language of the First Amendment also weighs in favor of interpreting the press clause as a structural protection. The amendment protects speech and the press. Speech is the product of speaking, and the constitutional protection extends to actors who are capable of speaking. The press, however, is not the product of any verb, it is a noun connoting a physical or structural entity. Historical evidence also supports this interpretation. For instance, in his draft Constitution for Virginia, Thomas Jefferson proposed the following language: "Printing presses shall be free."[35] Jefferson's reference to "printing presses" was to a structural entity—a means of communicating.

The Historical Basis for Interpreting the Press Clause as a Structural Provision

The history of the American press and of the First Amendment supports an interpretation of the press clause as a structural provision. It also further demonstrates the nature of the press clause's structural concerns. Indeed, historical evidence suggests that the drafters of the First Amendment wanted to protect a certain type of press industry—one that was competitive, participatory, political, and with low barriers to entry.

The physical operations of a colonial printing press also illustrate how the constitutionally protected press acted as a community communications forum. Printers set up printing presses that essentially served as bulletin boards for the community. The printer was dependent upon the community for providing news or opinions to place in the newspaper. Editors believed that their papers should serve as forums for airing political debate, so the contents of the newspapers tended to focus on political opinion essays contributed by subscribers. As Arthur Schlesinger concludes, the revolutionary press was primarily a transmitter of public opinion.[36]

The opposition to particular kinds of restrictions placed on the colonial and revolutionary newspapers further indicates the framers' structural views of a free press. Newspapers opposed the British Stamp Act and the proposed postal restrictions in 1792; both these measures in effect placed a tax upon the circulation and dissemination of newspapers—structural functions vital to the survival of a press industry. Printers had also protested the licensing system which had been brought over from Britain. Perhaps the strongest colonial argument against licensing was that the licensing system perpetuated monopolies in the printing press industry. Licensing constituted an interference with the fluid and competitive structure of the press.

Protests over these restrictions demonstrated that Americans wanted an open and competitive newspaper industry. Also, the unrestricted circulation of newspapers appears to have been more important than freedom from persecution for seditious libel. The framers seemed to be more concerned about getting ideas out into the public than about the particular content and quality of those ideas. For instance, colonial and revolutionary newspapers tended to print rumor and emotional propaganda. However, as long as there were enough newspapers to permit a full array of ideas to circulate among the public, the publication of some rumor and propaganda did not seem to pose a problem for the framers. They apparently were more concerned with having outlets for publishing their own ideas than with ensuring that whatever ideas were printed were of a particular quality or content.

The view that the press clause was designed to protect the structure of the newspaper industry rather than the content of the particular speech is consistent with the status of the common law of seditious libel. Even eighteenth-century printers generally accepted the law of seditious libel; some editors favored prosecutions for such libel at some times and not at other times. However, they all protested restrictions on a competitive press industry.

Conclusion

The press clause differs significantly from the speech clause, and these differences reveal the identity and nature of the press as protected by the First Amendment. It protects a press that serves the needs of a democratic society and government. The press clause as a structural provision seeks to preserve a competitive, participatory, and independent identity of the press industry as a whole. Thus, because the new media technologies of the twenty-first century have these same qualities, they seem especially qualified for First Amendment protection.

10

The Press, Politics, and the Democratic Dialogue

BECAUSE THE PRESS clause of the First Amendment has a close connection with the democratic process, the constitutional definition of a free press should incorporate the political values of a free press. A constitutionally protected press is one that serves democracy; consequently, the constitutional definition of the press rests on the press functions that are vital to the integrity and functioning of democratic government.

As discussed in the previous chapter, the press in a democracy must serve three functions:

1. the truth function, where the press acts as a forum through which society can discover the kind of social truth needed to govern itself;
2. the watchdog function; and
3. the democratic dialogue function, which serves society's need to build democratic institutions through interactive social communication and debate.

The new media technologies seem especially suited to this third function. Yet even if they perform any of the three press functions, they should qualify for constitutional protection.

The first two functions have received judicial recognition in previous First Amendment cases and have been advanced frequently by the press in claims for greater constitutional freedoms. The fourth estate model addresses both the truth and the watchdog functions, but it totally ignores the democratic dialogue function. Moreover, the courts have never specifically incorporated the democratic dialogue function into any constitutional press doctrine, and the modern mass media, while striving to serve the truth and watchdog values, has largely ignored the democratic dialogue function—a function that characterized the eighteenth-century American press.

Any future press model or definition should not only incorporate the dialogue function, but must also continue to recognize the truth and watchdog functions, even though the watchdog function is increasingly being performed by various political interest and constituency groups like Common Cause and the National Organization for Women (NOW).

The democratic dialogue function requires a participatory press, much like the one that existed in the late eighteenth century. According to John Dewey's theory of democracy, participation in community life is an essential condition for a healthy democracy. Such communal involvement requires the public's participation in political dialogue, a prerequisite for action and for the formation of the political association necessary for democratic politics. Social dialogue is also necessary for achieving the kind of popular consent vital to a democracy. For such consent to have a moral value, it must be an informed consent preceded by a public debate in which all have the opportunity to participate. Therefore, an accessible and participatory communication system through which popular consent can be formed constitutes a necessary condition for democracy.[1]

The twentieth-century media, however, has not followed the Dewey participatory model. Instead, it has exhibited a distrust of public opinion and participation and has adopted the Lippmann model of journalism, which is based on the premise that government should be run by knowledgeable experts, whose access to reliable information immunized them against the emotional stereotypes that dominated public debate. Walter Lippmann had little use for public debate; in his view, most political questions were too complex to be submitted to popular judgment.[2] Lippmann's ideas provided a founding charter for modern journalism and an elaborate rationale for a journalism guided by a new ideal of professional objectivity. The role of the press, to Lippmann, was to circulate information, not to encourage debate.

Lippmann's position put him at odds with Dewey, who believed that the search for reliable information is itself guided by the questions that arise during public arguments about a given course of action. According to Dewey, the knowledge required by any community emerges only from open social debate. Thus, the distinguishing mark of democracy is one that extends the circle of that debate as widely as possible, which is accomplished most effectively through a participatory press.

Lippmann's distrust of the public and his advocacy of an aloof and objective press previewed a similar distrust reflected in the fourth estate model of the press. By seeing itself as the public's agent in the political process, with the duty of investigating and checking government abuses, the modern press has further abandoned its role as a forum for social conversation. Much of the press, in its eagerness to inform the public, has overwhelmed society by delivering an abundance of indigestible facts whose relevance often remains unrecognized by the general public. The problem is not one of insufficient information, but of assimilation of information, which can only occur with debate. Yet as the media has evolved according to the Lippmann model into a fourth estate, it has inhibited the public from participation in a social dialogue through the press.

Following the Lippmann model, the modern media acts as a conduit of information produced by journalists and knowledgeable experts. Journalists, for instance, tend to overwhelmingly choose experts as their sources. Dan Hallin notes that viewers are twice as likely to see think-tank academics and other freelance political experts interviewed on network news as viewers are to see average voters. In fact, the presence of voters in campaign coverage has declined from more than 20 percent of sound bites in 1972 to no more than 4 percent in 1988.[3] Yet as voters have been pushed out of the political debate, they have also turned away from the voting booth.

The decline of public dialogue and debate is a glaring side effect of the fourth estate press. By factoring the public out of the media dialogue, the press gives exclusive focus to journalists and their sources. Rather than encouraging public debate, the press simply reports about the public; thus, in seeking to build audiences the press often becomes more an entertainer than a public communications forum. In so doing, the press may only intensify the increasing isolation felt by individuals in society. And communal occasions have so faded from contemporary society that the importance of the press as a source of communal dialogue and experience becomes all the more important.

Sociologists proclaim that people are in search of some kind of community involvement—the kind that often begins with involvement in community conversation. Some scholars attribute the dissolution of community bonds to the absence of a common language or conversation to express a community identity and to transcend individualism.[4] The current popularity and glut of television talk shows reveals a society in need of some kind of community conversation: Phil Donahue, Oprah Winfrey, Geraldo Rivera, Sally Jessy Raphäel, Joan Rivers, Regis and Kathie Lee, Jenny Jones, Jay Leno, Arsenio Hall, David Letterman, Conan O'Brien, Montel Williams, Chuck Woolery, John Tesh, and Ricki Lake. This long list has significantly grown from the Johnny Carson and Merv Griffin days. With many of these shows encouraging audience participation, the talk show has become a kind of group therapy and social dialogue—the kind the mainstream press no longer encourages.[5]

Without intelligent social conversation, a meaningful democratic community is nearly impossible to achieve. In modern society, the press offers perhaps the most effective forum for such conversation, and, not surprisingly, the absence of a participatory press has coincided with a politically apathetic and alienated public. A recent study concludes that citizens believe that their political system has been usurped by the media, which often ignores the concerns that citizens want addressed. It also found that social communication moves between centers of power—the media, the government, and powerful lobbyists—and often bypasses the public. Thus, a disillusioned public sees the media as an aloof institution impervious to the long-term interests of the nation, manipulating the democratic discourse in a way that treats people as consumers to be entertained rather than citizens to be engaged.[6]

The decline in twentieth-century American politics has received enormous attention. Many political scientists have concluded that the ''decline in the partisan behavior of voters and the decline in media partisanship have reinforced one another.'' Unfortunately, the mere extension of voting rights and opportunities cannot overcome the political alienation felt by citizens nor can they sponsor the kind of public debate that motivates participation in politics.[7] A connection between politics and community provided by the press is what is needed.

As a result of the Lippmann or fourth estate model, the press has acted like a lecturer speaking to a classroom full of passive observers. But at the end of the lecture the press walks out, leaving the audience to ponder in silent isolation the contents of the lecture. Yet if there is to be action resulting from the lecture, if the subject of the lecture is to end up a matter of public policy, then the audience must become engaged in debate and discussion on the subject. All good speakers know that the first step in becoming involved in an issue is by opening up a question-and-answer period after the lecture. Often the liveliest part of the lecture, it is also the best time for the audience to digest the material. The media frequently gives its audience a lecture, but it rarely encourages a question-and-answer period following that lecture. That is the challenge to a participatory press.

The recognition of the decline of political discourse and the shortcomings of a fourth estate model of the press, along with a desire to reinvigorate American democracy and the social dialogue, has brought a resurgence of interest in Dewey's model of a participatory press. Scholars argue that the achievement of a participatory democracy requires that the public "pay attention" to the institutions that support democracy. Not only does the press constitute such an institution, it is the primary forum through which a democratic public "pays attention" to its democratic institutions.[8]

The press is one of the few nongovernmental institutions through which communities and individuals can engage in the language and civic association of a democratic culture. Since the press is the most obvious community communication channel, it directly affects the functioning of other community institutions. A 1988 study has shown that the quality of community communication channels greatly contributes to the quality of life in those communities and the functioning of public institutions there. Studies also show that local media are often assumed to have a major role in encouraging a sense of community identity and in helping public opinion form on community issues.[9]

Daniel Yankelovich likewise argues that the health of democracy in the United States depends on achieving a more engaged and thoughtful public dialogue. Unlike most who decry the quality of American public opinion, however, he emphasizes the limits of information in remedying this situation. While facts and information on political problems abound, judgment and public opinion on those problems are sorely lacking. Yankelovich describes public judgment as the state of highly developed public opinion that exists once people have engaged an issue, considered it from all sides, understood the choices, and accepted the full consequences of the choices they make. He uses the example of the nation's health care system: For years the press has run stories about the extent of the problem and the alternative solutions; yet this information has, to date, failed to produce any political consensus on the problems, and the absence of public dialogue through the press has in turn contributed to an absence of public opinion or judgment on the matter. With his faith in public debate, Yankelovich returns to the Dewey model of the press and participatory democracy.[10]

Similarly, James Fishkin argues that the public has failed to form opinions on about 80 percent of the issues. Traditional polling does not allow those polled to discuss the issues, nor does the media facilitate any kind of meaningful public dialogue. Therefore, Fishkin urges the media to involve the public more in the political dialogue and deliberative process. As media scholar James Carey argues, "The public will begin to reawaken when they are addressed as a conversational partner and are encouraged to join the talk rather than sit passively as spectators before a discussion conducted by journalists and experts."[11]

Democracy thus needs the sharing of opinions as much as it needs the sharing of objective information. Opinion is the great equalizer of society; only the experts have access to the complex information relative to society's problems, but everyone can form opinions. Yet only through the sharing of opinions can society bring the experts and the public together. A social dialogue that ignores opinion will exclude and alienate the public from politics and public decision making.[12]

A participatory press, like that which existed in the eighteenth century, is one of the primary means for sharing and developing public opinion. Without such a press, society lacks dialogue and debate. Mary Ann Glendon, in discussing the decline in political debate, argues that the prominent places for political discussion, such as television, give little attention to public issues and provide even less public engagement in whatever discussions do exist. Likewise, according to one newspaper editor, the modern press "must take part of the blame for a nationwide trend toward orthodoxy and dryness in public discussion."[13]

In addition to news and information, the public must also have the opportunity to debate their implications concerning public policy. Only through such debate can the public reach a real reckoning with its political problems. The savings and loan crisis exemplifies an issue that became news but never became a subject of debate. Perhaps that is why the public seems to refuse to make sacrifices or to accept bad or painful news—they are left out of the deliberative process. Yet as public discourse diminishes, public problems grow ever more obscure, making it possible, for instance, for the S&L debacle—one of the biggest scandals in U.S. history—to pass relatively unnoticed through the political system. As Jay Rosen notes, public dialogue and discourse is also diminishing because it is becoming so expensive, since television has become our primary forum for political discussion. Although television provides news through its various news and information programs (neatly prepared and coordinated with advertisers), it cannot provide the time and space for the kind of public discourse that characterized the eighteenth-century press.[14]

Social critic Christopher Lasch argues that the kind of information essential to democracy can be generated only by vigorous popular debate. When people engage in arguments that grab their attention, they become avid seekers of relevant information. Otherwise, people take in information passively, if they take it in at all. The role of the press is to encourage debate, not simply to supply the public with information. The public knows less about public affairs than it used to know, but since they no longer participate in debates on national issues, the public may have less reason to be better informed. When debate becomes a lost art, information makes no impression.[15]

History demonstrates that a participatory press is vital for a healthy democracy and for political activism and reform. Periods of intense political activity accompany or follow times in which a participatory press thrives. The eighteenth-century movement for independence and nationhood was sparked by a highly participatory and partisan press. Historians conclude that American democracy was "fostered by the communications media at the time."[16]

The election of Thomas Jefferson to the presidency ushered in a democratic movement in which national power was transferred from the elitist Federalists to the more democratic-minded Jeffersonian Democrats; and the intense democratic activity of the Jacksonian period coincided with a vibrant partisan and participatory press. Press historians suggest that "the appearance of the penny press and the rise of the common people in the Jacksonian democracy were closely integrated." The new papers "were spokesmen for egalitarian ideals in politics, economic life, and social life." As politics filled the contents of the highly partisan newspapers, those newspapers in turn served as the principal weapons in the intense partisan battles of the age.[17]

The next great period of democratic activity and reform occurred in the late nineteenth century during the Populist movement. Lawrence Goodwyn argues that populism was the largest and most intense mass democratic movement in American history. During that period, the press flourished and 80 percent of the eligible voters typically voted in presidential elections. Late-nineteenth-century journalism served as an extension of the town meeting. Newspapers created a public forum in which the issues of the day were hotly debated. The number of daily newspapers quadrupled and the number of copies sold each day increased almost sixfold. A similar advance was being made by weekly newspapers.[18]

In the late nineteenth century, the mainstream press was being transformed by the emergence of a "new journalism," exemplified by the enormous success of Joseph Pulitzer's *New York World*. The "new journalism" was characterized by the opinionated feature of the newspapers and the unique identity that each derived from its editorial posture. For instance, the Scripps newspapers reflected a spirit of working-class protest that was inherent in the character of their owner-editor, Edwin Wyllis Scripps.[19]

More so than the mainstream press, an emerging Populist

press energized the political climate of the era. The Populist news-papers united in the National Reform Press Association, which became the propaganda arm of the Populist party in the early 1890s. More than one thousand Populist newspapers started up in the 1890s. The National Reform Press Association stood as a monument to the democratic intensity of the agrarian crusade and provided the adhesive for the democratic Populist movement. As a participatory press, it strove to be a continuing democratic di-alogue between rank-and-file members and elected spokesmen.[20]

In addition to the National Reform Press Association, the im-migrant press in late–nineteenth- and early–twentieth-century America also revealed the importance of a participatory and com-munity-responsive press. This press helped new immigrants as-similate into American life and influence public policy. The Nor-wegian-American press, for instance, actively sought to shape the political and social opinions of its readers. The Jewish newspa-pers in America, highly opinionated and political in their con-tents, likewise helped to Americanize the new immigrants and served as a communication channel among the Jewish communi-ties. The most influential and widely read Yiddish newspaper, *The Forward,* functioned less as journalism than as dialogue within the immigrant community."[21]

The decline of the Populist press after the 1896 election oc-curred at the same time that centralization and corporate domi-nation of mass communications began to take hold. A commer-cialized press practicing the objectivism espoused by Lippmann replaced an opinionated, participatory press that helped build the American commitment to democratic politics. With mergers and chain-ownership, the newspaper business gradually became, like other aspects of commerce, centralized big business.[22] With the demise of a participatory and opinionated press, Americans began to feel increasingly distant from their government. It is no acci-dent that popular participation in politics reached its height during the late nineteenth century when partisan and opinion journalism flourished.

The intense democratic activity of the late nineteenth century was revived again in the 1960s with the civil rights, antiwar, and social protest movements. The surge of political reform affected nearly all areas of American life, including the political process.

Voting rights laws were passed, the voting age was lowered, election procedures and campaign finance laws were changed to lessen the influence of special interest, and reapportionment laws were modified so as to achieve the democratic ideal of "one person, one vote."

Despite the fact that the media had become highly concentrated into corporate conglomerates, new press entities arose which helped to foster and encourage the political activism of the 1960s. Magazines like *Harper's* and *Atlantic Monthly* took a reinvigorated interest in public affairs during the 1950s and 1960s. Opinion journals like *National Review, The Nation, The Reporter, The Progressive, The New Leader,* and *The New Republic* enlivened the political debates of the era. Furthermore, the expansion of the religious press also intensified political debate.[23]

The "underground press" movement that swelled to prominence in the 1960s helped to motivate many of the social and political movements of the 1960s. Underground papers reflected a rebellion not only against the "establishment" but also against the conventional mass media. The most effective underground newspapers "did a capable job of criticizing both and of breathing new life into the dead-center American social and political scene of the 1960s." An estimated 457 underground newspapers circulated during the 1960s, in addition to approximately 3,000 underground high-school papers.[24] Perhaps the best known of the underground newspapers was the *Village Voice,* founded in 1955. In addition, new journals and newspapers that started up during this era included *Rolling Stone, Ms., The Black Panther, Essence, Black Enterprise,* and *Black Collegian.* Furthermore, neighborhood newspapers and newsletters sponsored by nonprofit organizations also started appearing in greater numbers during the social unrest of the 1960s. Such publications appeared to focus on problems that were defined by neighborhood residents and often helped unite residents to take action on those problems.[25]

The connection between democratic activism and a vibrant, participatory, and opinionated press was further demonstrated during the international democratic movements of the late 1980s and early 1990s. The revolutions in Eastern Europe and the Soviet Union were influenced and strengthened by a democratically inspired press, and the Tiananmen Square protest in China resulted from the promptings of a new press committed to democracy.

The lessons of history show that if the First Amendment is to support democracy, it must protect a press that in turn supports democratic processes—a participatory press. In a democracy, the press must not only inform the reader, it must also involve the audience in a public debate and facilitate a democratic dialogue of opinions. There are three steps to political action: people must be informed, they must feel consulted and then form judgments through communication, and they must form a commitment to action. While the fourth estate press may serve the first step, only a participatory press can fulfill the second and third. Such a press will also strengthen American pluralism by helping minorities express themselves and assimilate in their own way into society.

Given the democratic role of the press and the lessons from history, a model or definition of the press begins to emerge. The eighteenth-century experience shows that a democratic press should be a participatory press that encourages and facilitates political debate and discourse. The nineteenth century demonstrates that the press should be democratic in its scope—namely, that it should reach out to the whole community and be available to all members of the community. And the twentieth century has shown that the press should also provide accurate and objective reporting about public issues. Therefore, the press of the next century must be clarified in such a way that all these functions are recognized.

The new media technologies promise to provide the kind of citizen interaction and dialogue that occurred in the eighteenth-century press and to provide access to a wider public than ever before. But the challenge ahead is to shape First Amendment doctrines that will facilitate such a transformation to a more participatory and democratic press. Constitutional protection should be accorded to the new media technologies that exert a positive influence on the democratic process, particularly on collective deliberation and democratic participation.

PART V

The Future of the First Amendment

Given the dramatic changes taking place in the press, as well as the outdated and inconsistent regulatory scheme currently governing the various types of media, the First Amendment doctrines in the future will have to be shaped to provide a uniform constitutional definition of the press. The only media industry to presently receive the full constitutional protection envisioned by the framers is the print media. However, industry analysts predict that the print technology of ink-on-paper will soon be replaced by an electronic form of delivery. Consequently, unless a technology-transparent definition of the press is reached, the American media of the future may be denied the constitutional protection it deserves.

11

Unifying the First Amendment for a Converging Press

THE AMERICAN PRESS stands at the brink of a period of substantial change. As with any prospect of change and technological progress, a spirit of optimism and anticipation prevails regarding the future press. Like most dramatic changes, however, growing pains often obstruct a smooth and predictable course of adjustment—and those pains have begun to be felt by the media.

The growing pains in the press have already caused fierce disputes over the future structure of the industry. These disputes involve the survival of various media entities and the activities and functions each will be free to perform. New technologies, new economic environments, new consumer tastes, and a new deregulatory approach of the FCC have fostered greater competition in the media industry. Then-FCC Chairman Alfred Sikes, for instance, predicted that the electronic media in the 1990s would witness greater competition and that there would be "a massive reduction in the entry barriers to electronic media."[1] Increased competition in an industry that has been somewhat insulated from competition, however, has obviously caused much anxiety and conflict.

As seen in the media wars emerging in Congress and at the FCC, the disputed issues involve the industry's structure and identity. The newspaper, cable and broadcast television industries, and the telephone companies and emerging computer communication technologies are all looking in various ways to the government to settle the conflicts and to bring a sense of harmony and structure to the communications field. Yet the disputes are not confined strictly to the regulatory arena—they are also spilling over into the courts. For instance, in response to the decisions of some telephone companies to exit the 900-number telephone service, the Information Providers Association announced their intention to litigate, accusing the phone companies of violating their First Amendment rights.[2]

The majority of disputes arising from the changing media will involve more press issues than speech issues. Instead of speech content, the primary concern will be one of industry structure and organization. Yet like most media conflicts and disputes of the past, and particularly those brought to a legislative or regulatory tribunal, the future disputes over industry structure will inevitably involve the courts and, ultimately, the First Amendment. As they address these disputes, the courts will have to forge new First Amendment doctrines. With the press already redefining itself, the courts and the First Amendment will eventually have to catch up to this change of identity. As history has demonstrated, press technologies and practices exert a strong influence on the development of communications law and First Amendment doctrines.

The Supreme Court has had few opportunities in the past to define the press, primarily because the press has been a fairly static industry and because previous press cases have involved the activities and not the identity of the press. Yet even on those rare occasions, the Court has had difficulty in articulating a definition. In *Branzburg v. Hayes,* 408 U.S. at 704, for instance, Justice Byron White said that any effort to define the press "would present practical and conceptual difficulties of a high order." Scholars have echoed this sentiment: "It is unlikely that we will succeed in defining the press in ways which will prove satisfactory." Yet with the rapidly changing press industry and the emergence of new and complicated communications technologies, the need to define the press is greater than ever before.[3]

Not only has the Court not constitutionally defined "the press," it has not even clearly distinguished the press clause from the speech clause. Despite a flurry of interest in a suggestion by Justice Potter Stewart that the press clause did have meaning apart from the speech clause, "neither the Supreme Court nor any other court found within the clause anything not already available in the speech clause."[4] Undoubtedly, the hesitancy to give independent meaning to the press clause results from the absence of any fundamental and clear understanding of what constitutes "the press." Although some of the Court's decisions in the 1970s implied a tentative acceptance of the fourth estate view of the press, that view is clearly inadequate for the future.

Without a definition of "the press," the courts cannot articulate the press protections of the First Amendment and apply them to the emerging media technologies. Moreover, as the media undergoes rapid change, the existing confusion regarding First Amendment press protections only escalates. For instance, new electronic media are often profoundly different in character from either of the more traditional forms of broadcast or print. In addition, interactive video and computer communication defy conventional notions of "publishing." In this radically new environment, in which telephone companies claim a constitutional right to "publish" over their own lines and cable companies liken themselves to newspapers, it becomes exceedingly urgent to ask how traditional First Amendment legal standards should be applied to these new kinds of media. Should each medium be considered a "law unto itself," as the Supreme Court declared long ago?[5] Or should Congress, the courts, and the FCC try to develop a more coherent, integrated legal framework? These questions depend fundamentally on the First Amendment rights of the various media, which in turn depend on whether those media qualify as a First Amendment press.

The failure to broadly define the press has in the past often led to a failure to consider the First Amendment when new communications technologies have been introduced and subsequently regulated. Indeed, the First Amendment has often been ignored when new communications technologies have been initiated. For instance, telegraph law was modeled on a nineteenth-century law that regulated the railroads. Consequently, the First Amendment was almost totally absent from cases concerning telegraphy. Without concern for First Amendment values, Congress regulated theh telegraph under the commerce clause, just as it had the railroads.[6] Because the early telegraph carried so few words at such a high cost, people thought of it not as a medium of expression but as a business machine. No one initially used telegrams for debate and self-expression. Therefore, the courts did not perceive this new technology of communication as an extension of the printed word, sharing the same significance and the same need for protection as the print media. The courts later applied the precedents of telegraphy and common carrier law to the telephone, which was seen as a successor to the telegraph. Once again, Congress and the courts did not view the telephone as a successor to the printing press. And there was a glaring absence of any mention of the First Amendment in the early court decisions involving regulation of the telegraph and telephone.

The broadcast industry suffered a similar fate. The fear of spectrum scarcity and monopolistic corporations overshadowed the concerns of the First Amendment. Consequently, by 1934 a major medium had come to be licensed, regulated, and even censored. Contrary to the First Amendment's mandate of "no law" abridging freedom of the press, Congress had made such a law and set up the FCC to implement it. Like the regulation of the telephone and the telegraph, the Communications Act of 1934 was based on the commerce clause of the Constitution. Even though the First Amendment had removed from the jurisdiction of Congress one significant area of interstate commerce, namely the exchange of ideas through the press, broadcast regulation "was conceived, was adopted and took hold in an era when the scope of the First Amendment was largely undefined."[7]

The Supreme Court found no constitutional dilemma in a system of regulated broadcasting. In 1940, it sustained the constitutionality of the Communications Act of 1934 without any consideration of the First Amendment. Licensing in the public interest was rationalized for broadcasting by the need to protect the spectrum from monopolists and to ensure spectrum clarity. In short, two things were true about broadcast regulation that were not true for print: first, government entered the business of licensing the broadcast press, and second, government began monitoring the content of programming to determine whether the broadcaster was fulfilling the obligations of a public trustee. Thus, within the meaning of the First Amendment, the broadcast media did not qualify as "the press."

The regulation of both telephone and broadcasting has resulted largely from a fear of monopoly control. For instance, the debates over the 1927 Radio Act, which constituted the first instance of broadcast regulation, reflected an intense opposition to the broadcasting activities of AT&T—the giant of American industry. As a result, the Radio Act penalized AT&T by restricting cross-ownership of telephone companies and broadcasting stations, which at the time were small and struggling, unable to match the economic power of AT&T. Such regulations suggest that the development of media law may owe more to a hostility to monopolists than to a concern for the fulfillment of First Amendment values.[8]

Once the broadcast media was regulated, the government naturally became committed to furthering its regulatory scheme. Cable technology's effort to enter the market in the 1960s ran headlong into this scheme. intensified the struggle. As long as the FCC had a commitment to the continued vitality and existence of the regulated television broadcasting system, it would not tolerate the introduction of any new technology that might undermine that regulatory method.

Just as telephones were treated as telegraphs, cable was linked with broadcast television. Yet from a constitutional point of view, cable and broadcast television were substantially different. Television, as broadcast over the air, used "scarce" spectrum rationed by the government. Cable, on the other hand, did not use any such limited broadcast spectrum. Nonetheless, when the FCC regulated cable, the Supreme Court found no constitutional problem, just as it had found none with broadcast television. In fact, the regulation of cable was seen as ancillary to the FCC's regulation of television broadcasting. The First Amendment question about whether government may regulate one medium of expression just because that medium in some way affects another regulated medium was not confronted.[9]

Fears and suspicions of new media technologies have historically inspired regulation of those technologies. According to Donald Lively, the fear of a "new medium's 'potential for evil' has been a consistent rationale for either denying new media First Amendment recognition or circumscribing their First Amendment freedom." Such fears and mistrust of new media are not historically unusual. Gutenberg's printing technology was criticized for its potential for producing popular books that would distract the reading public from the Bible. Much later, when rotary printing was introduced in the nineteenth century, leading eventually to the penny press, there was great indignation at its vulgarity. In the 1930s, publishers were so afraid of the emerging radio industry that they threatened to lobby Congress for legislation restricting it.

The current system of government regulation has resulted from the fear that the media is "fraught with possibilities for service of good or evil."[10] Implicit within this regulatory scheme, which is constitutionally inapplicable to the print media, is the assumption that newer media have, according to Lively, "improper or indecent tendencies or powers of persuasion that the original press lacked" (p. 1075). There has been a continuing reluctance to admit the legitimacy and positive contribution of any new medium or to see the press implications of technological developments. When sound was introduced into motion pictures, musicians' associations agitated publicly that sound movies were a destructive social force. From the infancy of radio, newspapers feared the impact of broadcasting on their economic survival. Exhibiting a more profound fear of radio, researchers noted after its introduction that "parents have become aware of a puzzling change in the behavior of their children." Years later, the surprising popularity of VCRs led social critics to conclude that America was becoming a recluse society.[11]

The initial reaction to motion pictures provides a good example of the social fears about new media technologies. In 1915, shortly after the introduction of motion pictures, the Supreme Court denied First Amendment status to that medium. Although decades later the Court reversed itself and recognized motion pictures as an important information source deserving of constitutional protection, yet the initial decision denying First Amendment status focused on motion pictures' "capability and power" for evil.[12] The Court concluded "that the potential for evil was greater in motion pictures than in print." Implicit in this distinction is the assumption that the public can better defend itself against offensive materials in the print media, but is vulnerable to subversive and dangerous messages transmitted by the electronic media.[13]

Like other new technologies, the telephone at first was also dismissed as frivolous at best and harmful at worst. A German psychiatrist accused it of literally driving people permanently insane, and some religious groups told their members not to use the telephone, which they believed was a device of Satan to make people lazy.[14] Today, the entry of new forms of telecommunication services and delivery systems, such as 900-number telephone services, raises similar fears. Clearly, there are some legitimate problems with this new medium, but many are based purely on fears relating to the changing role of the telephone. In the past, the telephone was mainly used for person-to-person conversations. Now it is becoming a mass medium in new and interesting ways—as demonstrated by 900 numbers—and in so doing threatens the more traditional mass media. According to one media scholar, "it is the traditional press publisher who is now trying to use the First Amendment as a justification for government regulation of other media speakers."[15]

The newer electronic and computer communications technologies, as with all new media before them, have also become the subject of reactionary attacks. Consistent with historical patterns, this hostile attitude comes partly from failing to recognize them as part of the legitimate press protected by the Constitution. Consider, for instance, an incident that took place in May 1990 involving a number of new computer bulletin boards. Armed with guns and search warrants, 150 Secret Service agents staged surprise raids in fourteen cities one morning, seizing forty-two computers and tens of thousands of floppy disks. The target of these raids was a loose-knit group of youthful computer enthusiasts suspected of trafficking in telephone access codes. Yet by attempting to crack down on telephone fraud, the federal agents shut down dozens of computer bulletin boards that may be as fully protected under the Constitution as the daily newspaper.[16] That protection, however, depends on whether computer bulletin boards qualify as "the press" under the First Amendment.

Several other recent conflicts involving new communications technologies have also raised the question of the constitutional definition of "the press." When subscribers to Prodigy, a 700,000-member information service, began posting messages protesting a rate hike, Prodigy officials banned discussion of the topic in the system's public forums. After protesters began sending private mail messages to other members and to advertisers, they were summarily kicked off the network. If Prodigy is like a newspaper, it is free to do this. But if it is eventually considered to be a common carrier that can exert no editorial control, it may not have such a freedom.

In perhaps the only court case to date involving such a computer bulletin board service, the court in *Cubby Inc. v. Compu-Serve Inc.,* 19 Med. L. Rptr. 1525 (S.D.N.Y. 1991), held that the bulletin board service exercised no editorial control over statements published by subscribers and hence could not be held liable for any of those statements found to be defamatory. Although the court did not attempt to broadly define "the press," its statements regarding the coming technological revolution are insightful:

> CompuServe and companies like it are at the forefront of the information industry revolution. High technology has markedly increased the speed with which information is gathered and processed; it is now possible for an individual with a personal computer and telephone line to have instantaneous access to thousands of new publications. . . . Technology is rapidly transforming the information industry. A computerized database is the functional equivalent of a more traditional news vendor, and the inconsistent application of a lower standard of liability to an electronic news distributor such as CompuServe than that which is applied to a . . . newsstand would impose an undue burden on the free flow of information. (1528)

Many information system designers view the now-tiny bulletin board system as the forerunner of a public computer network that will eventually connect every household across the country. The concern, however, is that legal precedents set today may hinder the future development of such promising communication systems. Consequently, future freedoms in the information age may depend on redefining our notion of "the press."

Unfortunately, because an overall definition of the press has not been reached, a confusing and inconsistent regulatory scheme has been created, with different regulations for different technologies. Each media form has been treated separately by the courts and the Congress. Taken as a whole, the press, as it comprises all the different media, is subject to a conflicting and confusing regulatory scheme. Freedom of the press, in turn, has evolved into a concept that varies with the nature of each medium.[17]

The print model of the First Amendment applies to the oldest of the media technologies—the printing press. This model is the most protective of the press and the most antagonistic toward any governmental regulation. The print model, however, was not carried over to the later technologies of telegraph, telephone, radio, or broadcast and cable television. When the telegraph and telephone came along, they were seen as natural monopolies, and the government began regulating them as it had been regulating the railroads—as monopolists that carried things other than messages.

Radio and broadcast television were treated differently. They resembled print in that someone was "publishing" something, as contrasted with the mere vehicular assistance to conversation rendered by the telephone. But because of the limited electromagnetic spectrum available for broadcasting, radio and television had some of the monopolistic character of a public utility. As a result, broadcast media acquired its own "hybrid" kind of regulatory scheme. It was regulated like a common carrier, but it was also treated like the print media in that it maintained some editorial control and enjoyed freedom from a mandated public right of access. Even though broadcasters were given some First Amendment rights, the FCC renewal of broadcast licenses rested on program content.

Courts have not viewed such governmental control of broadcasting as unconstitutional censorship, but as the equivalent of issuing a franchise to a utility based on public convenience and necessity. In addition to rules on content such as the Fairness Doctrine (which was eventually abolished in 1987) and ownership rules (which limited the number of newspapers and radio and television stations that any one entity could own), the broadcast model has tolerated significant licensing restrictions on each broadcast entity.

With three different media technologies, three models of regulation emerged: (1) the no-regulation model, developed for newspapers, magazines, and books; (2) the common-carrier model, which emerged later with the telephone and telegraph industry; and (3) the public trustee model, which governs the broadcast industries and incorporates the kinds of content regulation that would be impermissible if imposed upon books or newspapers. Still a fourth regulatory model has evolved with cable television. Like other new technologies, cable found itself under pervasive regulatory pressure before any national policy existed as to who should regulate it and what regulations were proper. Cable did not fit comfortably into the scheme established for carriers like telephone companies—entities historically indifferent to their messages and not thought to be engaged in speech or press activities protected by the First Amendment. Given its role of disseminating programming supplied by others, cable television did not exactly fit the mold of providers of original expression like newspapers and book publishers. Furthermore, the spectrum scarcity-based broadcast model did not suit a medium of potentially limitless channel capacity. Consequently, at the start of the 1970s, the FCC wanted a cable system that was partly a common carrier and partly a broadcaster, and it no longer wanted to stunt the growth of cable television but encourage growth in a controlled way. With these goals, the FCC adopted a new regulatory approach for cable.[18]

The present regulatory scheme for cable appears in the Cable Communications Policy Act of 1984. One of the primary features of the act is the franchising provision, which requires local franchises as a prerequisite to offering cable service. Franchisees receive an exclusive right to lay cable in a specific geographic area and to sell cable television services to the residents of that area. The act also mandates that the cable operator dedicate a number of channels for leased access. In addition to mandatory commercial access, the act allows local governments to require a cable operator to set aside channels for public and educational use. Finally, the cable act grants cities discretion to determine the number of cable operators that they will authorize in any particular geographic area. In particular, a city can choose to grant one exclusive franchise to one operator. The act, however, does not specify how the franchise selection process should operate. Not surprisingly, this exclusive licensing scheme has become a First Amendment battleground for excluded applicants.

The cable industry exists at a regulatory and technological nexus, somewhere between the broadcast industry and the telephone networks. Cable has similarities with the public trustee obligations of broadcasters, the natural monopoly of telephone companies, and the unregulated speech of the print media. Given its hybrid status, the courts have found it difficult to define the nature of cable's First Amendment protections. In *City of Los Angeles v. Preferred Communications, Inc.,* 476 U.S. 488 (1986), the Supreme Court held that cable systems have First Amendment "interests," but declined to specify the exact nature and extent of those freedoms. The Court has also never ruled on the legitimacy of public access requirements for cable.

Still a fifth type of regulatory approach may be emerging for the new electronic and computer technologies. Here again, the threat is that a new technology will spawn yet another model of regulation. However, fitting these new technologies into a regulatory scheme designed for some other kind of media also presents a problem. Giving new technologies such traditional labels as "broadcaster" or "common carrier" so as to determine their regulatory treatment tends to shape the evolution of these technologies as well as the way they are used and perceived. The expanding field of electronic publishing, for instance, forces a rethinking of old regulatory notions precisely because it combines aspects of print, cable, and telephone. From the viewpoint of most government regulators today, electronic publishing encompasses three separate systems: broadcast teletext, cable videotex, and telephone videotex. Currently, how an electronic text is regulated depends on whether it is delivered over broadcast television, a multipoint distribution system, an operational fixed-microwave service, direct broadcast satellite, telephone, or cable television.[19]

The current pigeonhole approach to media regulation often disposes of regulatory questions on a technology-by-technology basis, giving little attention to the new media's cumulative impact. In subsequently ruling on these regulatory schemes, the courts have persisted in searching for technological differences that in turn justify regulatory differences. This pursuit of classification, however, has forced "courts into the precarious, if not apostate, exercise of calibrating a medium's first amendment protection according to its 'peculiar characteristics.' "[20]

Computer bulletin board services represent another new technology that resides in a regulatory limbo. Are they common carriers, not liable for the content of the messages but also unable to interfere with that content? Are they broadcasters with a duty to offer some rights of access? Or should they be treated like the print media? Does *Phrack,* the electronic "newspaper" published on computer networks, qualify as the press and hence have constitutional immunity from the kind of government prior restraint and seizure of its files and equipment described in chapter 2?

The present multilayered regulatory approach to the media is not only inconsistent, but also encourages continual tinkering and fine-tuning by the government. It fosters, contrary to the spirit of the First Amendment, a constant government presence in the media. The broadcasting model especially requires such continual government attention. For instance, the FCC recently announced plans to significantly alter its regulations dealing with the programming ownership rights of the television networks. The current Financial Interest and Syndication Rules (also known as fin-syn rules or restrictions) bar television networks from owning rerun rights or partial financial interests in the programs they broadcast. The rules were intended to prevent the networks from using their access to prime-time television viewers as a stranglehold over producers and Hollywood studios. But as the audience share of the networks declines, such rules are seen as "just overregulation, burdensome regulation." Therefore, in April 1991, the FCC adopted new rules which partially relaxed the fin-syn restrictions by permitting networks to acquire financial interests and syndication in outside-produced programs subject to a two-step negotiation process. At the same time, the commission granted the Fox network an exemption from the fin-syn rules, allowing Fox to temporarily expand its broadcast schedule to eighteen and a half hours a week without becoming subject to these rules. Thus, as demonstrated by the complexity and instability of the fin-syn rules, the system of broadcast regulation requires continual government tinkering with the media.[21]

The current regulatory scheme facing the media also appears as a kind of interest-group patchwork of various concessions, regulations, and compromises to the various media groups.[22] In its regulatory stances, the FCC has continually tried to manipulate the balance of power among the various electronic media. Its regulations, such as the fin-syn rules, sometimes exist more as policy tools to assist favored industries than as directives of First Amendment values, and at the present time, the FCC seems focused on propping up an ailing broadcast industry. In easing the fin-syn rules, the FCC has also injected more competition into the business of producing prime-time television programming. The networks can now compete directly against the Hollywood studios and producers.

Currently, there is much talk about the decline and perhaps eventual death of broadcast television. Consequently, government has apparently begun trying to slow the development of cable, all in the interest of protecting broadcast television.[23] At the federal level, for example, the cable industry has been subjected to a roller coaster of regulation by the FCC and Congress. After deregulating cable in 1984, Congress reregulated it in 1992. Meanwhile, government continues its attempt to rescue broadcast television. During his term, FCC Chairman Alfred Sikes was apparently committed to advancing the interests of broadcast television; in attempting to help out the networks, for instance, the FCC considered eliminating the rule which prohibits the common ownership of cable television systems and national television networks.[24]

The FCC's regulatory treatment of the broadcast and cable television industries demonstrates an interest-group approach to structuring the media—an approach which may well intensify with the emerging media wars. So far, the FCC has tended to take an interest-group approach to the structural tensions between the networks, cable television companies, telephone companies, electronic publishing services, and television and motion picture producers. It has brokered out assorted duties and privileges to the various media groups in an attempt to create some sort of level playing field. According to Jonathan Emord, however, "any effort by government to help one group have access to the mass media is an act of censorship against another group, and any act by government to determine which people may have the privilege to engage in speech through any particular medium is a determination that some other people may not have that same privilege."[25] Therefore, the only way to truly protect a free press is to define the press not according to whatever companies are present in the media business, but according to the constitutional values and purposes of a free press. Without a consistent definition of "the press," the outcome of the escalating media wars will resemble more a brokered peace settlement than a lasting constitutional resolution.

The complex and confusing compartmentalization inherent in the current media regulatory scheme is also particularly inconsistent with and contradictory to the future media convergence. In an age of convergence, the question is whether each media should be considered as having a law unto itself or whether there should be uniform legal doctrines to support the technological convergence of the media. If newspapers are to be delivered electronically in the future, for instance, will they be regulated under the print model or the electronic model?

The convergence of communications technologies will tend to eliminate distinctions based on historical differences. A single physical means, such as wires or airwaves, may carry services that in the past were provided in separate ways. Conversely, a service that was provided in the past by any one medium, such as broadcasting, print, or telephone, in the future will be provided in several different physical ways. Consequently, the one-to-one relationship that used to exist between a medium and its use is eroding. Previously separate forms of communication are increasingly becoming part of one technologically indistinguishable system. Facsimile machines, for instance, combine the technologies of print and telephone. Therefore, given this technological convergence, judges and regulators should abandon the view that each medium is a separate forum with clearly defined differences and should instead recognize that information is disseminated from a variety of sources in the media marketplace and that "the influence of any one [medium] normally is balanced by the presence of others."[26]

Besides technological convergence, economic convergence has also occurred as media firms now commonly engage in several different ventures outside their traditional domains. Newspaper publishers no longer limit themselves to publishing newspapers, and television networks and station owners no longer just broadcast. Even telephone companies are now offering video programming to their customers. The increasing cross-ownership of dissimilar media into common hands has further undermined many reasons for treating each different media technology according to a different regulatory model. The recent rash of mergers in the communications industry has also reinforced media convergence. Thus, both technological convergence and economic convergence through cross-ownership have blurred the boundaries that once existed between companies publishing in the print domain—a domain fully protected by the First Amendment—and companies involved in other media businesses regulated by the government.[27]

This convergence of media obviously makes it more difficult to apply conventional definitions even to familiar technologies, much less to new technologies, and the nature of videotex demonstrates this convergence. Like cable, videotex resists classification according to the inherited scheme.[28] It resembles print by publishing words and graphics; it resembles broadcasting in that it is displayed on a video monitor; it resembles a common carrier because it is transmitted through telephone lines or coaxial cable. Furthermore, the convergence in communication technologies significantly changes the conditions under which the current maze of regulations was enacted. Media are now separated only by laws and regulations. And if the converging media is not accompanied by constitutional convergence, it may never be able to realize its potential, and the First Amendment may never keep up with a changing society.

Not only will the current regulatory pattern not work well in the future age of convergence, but it has not even worked well in the past. Numerous studies have shown that the current system of broadcast regulation possesses fatal flaws and should be eliminated. Other studies have argued that the regulation of the telecommunications industry is unjustified, since it is not a natural monopoly but one created by the regulations themselves. Likewise, although the FCC has traditionally sought to remedy the negative effects of the broadcasters' monopoly, it may in fact have strengthened that monopoly through its regulations. For instance, certain FCC rules blocking the licensing and construction of new television stations may have been responsible for the death of the DuMont Television Network in 1955.[29]

Government regulations and licensing standards have been blamed for encouraging television executives to avoid controversy and opinion. As John Seigenthaler of the Nashville *Tennessean* has put it, "television has been neutered by the FCC." Regulations have also been blamed for discouraging diversity and innovation in television programming. John Hendricks, the founder and chairman of the Discovery Channel, claims that Discovery was made possible only by the 1984 cable deregulation and that his new channel, the Learning Channel, "will face an uncertain future" if cable is reregulated.[30]

The regulation of broadcast and cable television has also produced an inhibiting or censorial effect on that media. In 1987, for instance, broadcasters, fearing retaliatory legislation regarding their license renewals, backed away from their First Amendment protections when they did not advocate repeal of the Fairness Doctrine. And the cable industry retreated from its victory in *Quincy Cable TV Inc. v. F.C.C.,* 768 F.2d 1434 (D.C. Cir. 1985), cert. den. 476 U.S. 1169 (1986). which held that rules requiring cable systems to carry signals of broadcasters in competitive markets were unconstitutional, because it was afraid that such strict First Amendment protection applied to cable would jeopardize the exclusive franchises enjoyed by cable operators.[31]

The current regulation of the media is further flawed by the multiplicity of government entities now involved in that regulation. The federal government primarily regulates the broadcast industry. Cable television, on the other hand, initially fell under local regulation. But with the 1984 Cable Act, the industry drifted under partial federal control. Nonetheless, with cable, cities have developed a taste for involvement in communications regulation, and many local telecommunications bureaucracies have sprouted. This regulatory appetite is extending to other new technologies with a local character, such as satellite master antenna television. It could further extend to videotex and teletext as well, if they evolve as primarily local services. Consequently, the desire of the new media industries to have well-defined, fairly uniform standards for programming is likely to clash with the increasing roles of state and local government in the new federalism of communications regulation.[32] Not only do new technologies face inconsistent regulatory schemes, they are also plagued with an insecurity over what level of government may be regulating them.

The cable industry provides a prime example of inconsistent regulation. In the span of one decade, the FCC in the 1980s virtually rescinded all of the rules it adopted in the 1970s. The 1984 Cable Act also shifted much of the regulatory authority over cable to local governments. Furthermore, the act seemed to rely more on the common carrier model than on the broadcast model, which had previously influenced earlier regulation of cable.[33] In 1992, Congress again reversed its course and called on the FCC to impose new regulations on cable.

The current regulatory scheme in which each medium is regulated differently has been criticized for encouraging what it was designed to combat—privilege, monopoly, and resistance to change. But few monopolies exist because of economic factors alone; they are usually sustained by the force of law. Such has been the case with governmental regulation of the media. Regulators have found it convenient to segregate activities and to keep each organization on its own turf. This segregation, however, has ensured monopolization.

The rigid delimitation of turf has greatly insulated the media from change and competition. Although monopolies may have made sense when communications networks were specialized in function and too expensive to duplicate, the new media and its technological convergence are gradually eliminating those conditions. Furthermore, there is a wide consensus that the existing regulatory structure has been rendered obsolete by the new electronic media. As recognized by Representative W. J. Tauzin, a member of the House telecommunications subcommittee, "the marketplace is changing under out feet completely, and we're going to have to do some quick-stepping to keep up with it." Cable television, for instance, has eliminated the scarcity rationale for the regulation of broadcasting. Moreover, the notion that the government may specify which communications entity is allowed to participate in which particular part of the information industry's vertical flow is hard to reconcile with the First Amendment.[34]

The constitutional challenge of the future is to formulate a definition of the press that transcends the communications technologies and the particular media interest groups and organizations existing at any one particular time. Indeed, "were one to create a limited definition for the term 'press,' it is quite conceivable that the Constitution would be incapable of withstanding the test of time."[35] A broad definition will not only prevent obsolete regulation, but will prevent the type of inconsistent regulation currently existing. Otherwise, the American constitutionally protected "free press" will continue to be subject to contradictory and haphazard government regulation.

This pervasive and yet somewhat random scheme of regulation is an obvious contradiction of the eighteenth-century–model press—a press free of any government licensing and regulation. Because only one type of press existed—the print press—it was easy to have a clear and unified view of the press and to avoid imposing contradictory regulations. Subsequently, however, the progress of technology clouded the vision of the press and of the First Amendment that had been so much clearer when only the print media existed.

Although many of the regulations are intended to counteract the effects of monopoly, they unfortunately have inhibited change and competition. While regulatory schemes incorporate a specific vision or assumption of the future identity and structure of the press, that identity is nonetheless quite uncertain, due to the unpredictable future of technological and consumer developments. Little of the current media structure was anticipated in 1984, when the Bell system was dismantled and Congress regulated the cable industry. Because it was assumed then that telephone and cable required different physical networks, the 1984 Cable Act mandated that these two industries be kept apart. Soon after 1984, however, technological developments allowed cable companies to offer wireless telephone service and telephone companies to provide television programming over their own networks. Likewise, many media analysts assume that the ideal future is a one-wire or one-carrier broadband switch, yet other experts predict that technological developments may be so rapid as to "leap-frog" the next expected level and move on to a more advanced technology. Thus, with the uncertainty of the technological and economic future, the continued maze of regulations may very well make the press a product of outdated governmental regulations rather than a product of technological progress and social desires.

The dangers of stifling regulations are especially acute, given the fresh opportunities for competition in the media. By the year 2000, for instance, it is predicted that there will be many sources of television programming, contrary to the situation in the 1970s when the three networks dominated the market. The delivery systems will also be varied—over-the-air, cable, video cassette recorder, multipoint-distribution systems—and high-powered, direct-broadcast satellites and fiber-optic cable may make a significant entry into television.

Many traditional media monopolies are giving way to more competitive arrangements. Television, for instance, is experiencing more competition on nearly every level. While the Fox Broadcasting Company added a fourth network, Paramount Communications Inc. and Time Warner each have announced plans to form a fifth and sixth network. In addition to the competition between the networks, cable has become a formidable competitor in the television programming field. What C-Span does for public service coverage, and CNN provides for foreign affairs viewing, the Discovery Channel contributes to other forms of "lifetime learning": history, nature, science, and technology. All of these alternative channels provide increasing competition for the large networks.

A recent FCC study concluded that the development of a fully competitive television marketplace is possible.[36] Clearly, local telephone companies are a strong potential competitor now that the courts have overturned legal restrictions prohibiting telephone companies from providing television programming over their networks. In January 1993, U.S. West announced plans to offer movies and other video services to its customers. Other potential competition looms from second cable systems and from such newer technologies as multichannel, multipoint distribution service (MMDS) and direct-broadcast satellites. The Competitive Cable Association (representing competing second systems) believes that competition could be dramatically accelerated if local municipal authorities who hand out franchises would abandon their monopoly franchising practices.[37] Multichannel, multipoint distribution services (which use over-the-air microwave transmissions and are familiarly referred to as "wireless cable") and direct-broadcast satellites are also being advanced as potential competitors to cable. Yet such competition may exist only if government policy does not skew the competition through outmoded regulation favoring one kind of technology over another.

The search for a unitary technology-transparent First Amendment theory to encompass both print and electronic media must start with a unified definition of the press, and the technological convergence of the media should provide a guide for the convergence of our constitutional definitions of the press. The introduction of new media technologies gives the courts an opportunity to articulate such a unified view of the press. In the 1970s, media law scholars predicted that the emergence of cable offered "an opportunity to develop a new constitutional theory consistent with the language and spirit of the First Amendment," but unfortunately that opportunity was not taken. Yet the arrival of still newer media technologies provides a second chance and "reintroduces the choice between media regulation and media protection and renews the question of whether freedom of the press should exist with or without regard to the form of the press."[38] Unless First Amendment doctrines finally catch up to a changing press, however, outdated regulations may stunt the growth of the media and the emergence of new technologies, thereby eliminating future opportunities to reshape constitutional press doctrines.

12

Applying the First Amendment to the New Press

PREDICTING CHANGE is a risky endeavor, but preparing for change is a necessity. And adequate preparation often requires an attempt at predictions. The forces of change emanating from the press will greatly influence the next period of evolution in First Amendment doctrines. Preparation for this constitutional evolution requires a prediction of the kinds of changes that will occur in First Amendment doctrines.

In defining the press and in adapting the First Amendment to new communication technologies, the courts will have to fashion a functional view of the press that will define it according to the constitutional values and purposes of a free press in a democratic society. Contrary to the fourth estate model advocated during the last evolutionary period in First Amendment press freedoms and which focused primarily on the watchdog function, the future definition of the press should also embrace the democratic dialogue function, one for which the new media technologies are particularly suited.

By taking a broader view of the press—one which envisions greater public participation made possible by new technologies—the courts will have to move away from a journalistic or interest-group view of the press clause. A broad definition of the press will in turn help to unify and harmonize the legal treatment of the various types of media and to dismantle the multitiered regulatory scheme currently governing the print, broadcast, and other electronic media. Finally, a definition of the press will more clearly delineate the boundaries of permissible and impermissible governmental regulation over the rapidly changing media and the newly emerging media technologies.

The constitutional recognition of the press has in the past simply rested on whatever press groups or technologies existed at the time and on whatever fears prevailed regarding the potential power of each medium. The courts have never defined the American press; they have only recognized assorted media groups according to various regulatory standards. This approach, however, ignores the constitutional aspect of the press. Constitutional law and values embody a kind of timeless, universal nature. Consequently, the press protected by the constitution must be a press that has a certain timeless definition or character. A mere recognition of established technologies and media organizations carries no such timeless or universal trait and hence fails to fulfill the constitutional mandate.

The First Amendment press clause strives to provide a consistent and predictable guide to a constantly changing American society—namely, that it must never abridge ''freedom of the press.'' Such a guide must outlive and oversee the continually changing field of communications technologies and the constant turnover of media actors. Mergers, acquisitions, bankruptcies, and the law of fluctuating fortunes exert a constant force of change in the media business, just as in any other business. Therefore, to hinge First Amendment protections on a mere recognition of the existing press, without reaching a broader constitutional definition of the press, will only guarantee obsolescence to the First Amendment.

Since a technological or institutional view of the press has proved to be inadequate, another method of definition must be pursued—one which focuses on the constitutional functions and role of the press in a democratic society. In this way, the press would be defined by what it does, rather than what it is. Such a definition is particularly valuable in an age of media convergence and changing press ownership, where some entities or corporations may be only partly engaged in press activities.

A functional definition of the press rests on the vital roles and functions performed by a free press (as described in chapter 9). An entity that performs any of those functions should qualify for protection under the press clause. This kind of functional definition guarantees that the press that is protected is the type of press needed by a democracy. As discussed earlier, this interpretation significantly distinguishes the press clause from the speech clause.

The press clause, as argued in chapter 10, is primarily concerned with supporting democracy. Although the speech clause protects all forms and content of individual expression, the press clause protects only a communications forum that serves certain essential democratic values: the attainment of political truth, the checking of government power and abuse, and the encouragement of public participation in democratic dialogue. This last value, in particular, applies to the newly emerging media technologies. Thus, to qualify for constitutional protection, a media organization must produce information or communication that has some political value or relevance. Furthermore, the organization or entity must facilitate group communication, not just a collection of private one-to-one communications.

The obvious problem with injecting a political requirement into the First Amendment press clause is one of discretion. There has always been a hesitancy to give judges any discretion in protecting constitutional liberties. The reality, however, is that they always exercise some discretion in deciding how to apply the law to the facts of any case before them. Furthermore, the proposed functional definition of the press does not provide unguided discretion—the courts must apply a three-part test to determine if any media entity is performing the truth, watchdog, or democratic dialogue function. Obviously, any entity providing a forum for radical political dissent should receive the strictest of First Amendment protections.

This functional definition of the press aims both to fulfill the values of the press clause and to release the First Amendment from the confines of technology. Just because the *National Enquirer* appears in traditional printed form should not automatically mean that it qualifies as a constitutionally protected press, particularly if it serves none of the political values of a free press and only strives to expose the private lives of movie stars and the lovers of Big Foot.

The framers protected the press because of its contribution to democracy. According to Bruce Owen, the First Amendment has at least one implicit assumption: that competition in the marketplace of ideas will be conducive to political freedom in a democratic system. Yet many critics claim that the media is producing a passive, disengaged citizenry that does not participate in elections or in public affairs. Though earlier in the country's history the needs of self-government demanded greater information disseminated to a wider public, the current needs focus on expanding the opportunities for communication and for engaging a wider public in the stream of social communication. Though the modern media has not met this need, perhaps the new technologies can; perhaps they can facilitate political action and reform just as the eighteenth-century press inspired colonists to break with Britain and to create a new democratic nation. Though Americans do not need to create a new nation, they do need to reinvigorate their democracy. And to do so, they need a vibrant and participatory press—one that is protected by the First Amendment.[1]

In focusing on a functional definition of the press, the new First Amendment doctrines should also concentrate on protecting communication itself rather than specific technologies. The press is not to be found within the walls housing the *New York Times,* but in the functions and activities performed by that newspaper. If an organization does not perform any constitutional function of the press, it should not qualify for constitutional designation as "the press."

It is altogether too easy to take an institutional or entity view of the press, rather than a functional one. Such a view looks at organizations or entities arbitrarily categorized as "the press" and then allocates constitutional protection among the various actors or entities involved in that press. The danger with an institutional view, however, is that it tends to freeze the current media industry and insulate it from social and technological change. Such a view also alienates the media from the public's communications needs and from the functions a press needs to perform in a democratic society.

An example of this kind of institutional or interest-group First Amendment approach is found in the recent Supreme Court decision in *Cohen v. Cowles Media Co.,* 111 S.Ct. 2513 (1991), where the Court found the media defendants liable for breaking a promise of confidentiality made to an informant who, as a political campaign worker, had provided the defendants with certain documents regarding criminal charges against the opposing party's candidate. In deciding the dispute, the Court weighed the interests of the three distinct groups involved—editors, reporters, and informants—and held in favor of the reporters and informants.[2] This actor-based or interest-group approach to the First Amendment, however, ignored both the function and the role of a free press in democracy. For instance, the Court's ruling sanctioned the withholding of important information from the public—that is, evidence of a smear campaign—and consequently frustrated the public's ability to make fully informed and reasoned political choices.[3]

In *Cohen,* the Court ignored the two principal functions of a free press—the search for truth and the support of self-government. The decision not only approved the withholding of truthful information, it punished the disclosure of information particularly relevant to the democratic process of self-government. Thus, treating the press clause as merely protecting certain actors in the press process rather than protecting certain essential functions of the press—the flow of information through society—led the Court in *Cohen* to a decision that penalized the values and functions of a free press in a democratic society.

Justice Harry Blackmun's dissenting opinion in *Cohen* rejected the majority's interest-group approach to the First Amendment. According to Blackmun's dissent, the press clause goes beyond protecting the rights of particular press participants and seeks to protect the free flow of truthful information necessary for the conduct of democracy. The dissent also demonstrates that an interest-group approach to the First Amendment contains the same problems as interest-group politics. As with interest-group politics, such an approach to the First Amendment ignores the broader picture, which includes the public interest and the role of the press in a democracy. An interest-group approach also weakens the connection between First Amendment law and any timeless constitutional values. Consequently, press freedoms increasingly come to have no solid constitutional basis; they are simply demands of a group.[4]

Unlike an interest-group approach, a functional definition of the press will broaden "the press" beyond the exclusive hold of journalists to include a wider, nonjournalistic public. A less limited press definition will in turn bring First Amendment press freedoms to a wider public. On several occasions, the Supreme Court has suggested such a broader identity of the press—an identity not confined to established media actors or entities. In *Lovell v. City of Griffin*, 303 U.S. 444 (1937), the Court held that the freedoms of the press were not limited to newspapers, and that, historically, the press comprehended "every sort of publication which affords a vehicle of information and opinion" (452). Later, in *Branzburg v. Hayes*, 408 U.S., 665 (1972), the Court stated that freedom of the press includes "the right of the lonely pamphleteer who uses carbon paper or a mimeograph as much as of the large metropolitan publisher who utilizes the latest photocomposition methods" (704).

Under the fourth estate view, the press was basically equated with the journalist. The challenge both to the press and to First Amendment doctrines in the coming decade, however, is to include and embrace a wider public. Such a view of the First Amendment would correspond with the workings of the eighteenth-century press and would surely accommodate the emerging media technologies. As Lawrence Grossman, former president of NBC News and the Public Broadcasting Service, argues,

> Democracy will best be served in the 21st century by returning to the 18th-century idea of an independent and totally unregulated press, a press that is controlled by many different owners, a press that offers access to many different voices, and a press that makes available essential public affairs, educational and cultural programming to all our citizens.[5]

A broadening of the definition of "the press" effectively increases opportunities for access and diversity.

In the simplicity of its language, the press clause protects "the press." It does not specifically or exclusively protect reporters, editors, or even journalists in general. When the First Amendment was adopted in 1791, journalism as a profession did not exist. What the drafters did protect with the press clause is illustrated by the kind of press that existed in late–eighteenth-century America. Eighteenth-century printers frequently published local newspapers by themselves, without a staff of editors or reporters. The role of news gathering was left up to their readers, who would contribute local news, essays, and opinions about public issues.

Taking a historical view of the First Amendment, and considering the function of a press in a democratic society, it becomes apparent that the constitutional definition of the press is far broader than simply consisting of the functions of modern journalists. Although perhaps only journalists can perform the watchdog function of a free press, they cannot fulfill the democratic dialogue role. Yet as telecommunications, computer networks, and interactive television technologies encourage a more personal and participatory communications system, they should not have to confront First Amendment doctrines shaped, for instance, in response to the dominating media role played by the large newspapers or the three television networks. Economic regulations facing these new communications technologies should therefore be evaluated in light of the First Amendment's concern with a competitive, participatory press. Perhaps the greatest obstacle facing these new technologies will not be restrictions on source confidentiality or freedom from subpoenas, but economic regulations which thwart their chances for survival and growth. Such obstacles resemble those faced by colonial printers when confronted with licensing and taxation restrictions.

There is much controversy over how the First Amendment will be applied to emerging communications technologies. Many lawyers and journalists try to envision the specific effects on the content and quality of information that will result from the various new media technologies and from diverse regulatory schemes. They advocate certain regulations based on their fears of the kind of speech a certain unregulated media might communicate. They also debate the future course of libel and copyright law as they may pertain to the new media. But before determining what expressions and information may be produced in the future, and before deciding what press freedoms the media of the future will have, "the press" must be constitutionally defined. There can be no debate about the effects of government regulations prior to determining the nature of the press which is immune under the First Amendment from regulatory infringement.

In advocating a unified First Amendment theory, which may now be possible with a unified means of technological delivery,

Henry Geller promotes scrapping the current broadcast regulatory scheme. Many scholars similarly argue that different First Amendment theories for print and electronic media in general should not exist; they see no legitimate justification for medium-specific theories of the First Amendment. The argument is that government should consider the entire media environment when making communications policy. Only by reaching a constitutional definition of the press, however, will the current inconsistent and multitiered regulatory scheme facing the media be eliminated.[6]

In broadly defining the press according to its democratic functions, and especially considering the democratic dialogue function, it is clear that the new media qualifies as the press. Technologies like computer bulletin boards and telephone information services definitely serve the function of promoting a participatory social communication forum. According to Leonard Sussman, new information systems like videotex should be regarded as "the press" that is protected by the First Amendment, and not seen as a common carrier without First Amendment protection.[7]

In many ways, the new technologies may allow a return to the communication model of the eighteenth-century printers. Technologies such as electronic mail service, computer network services, and computer bulletin boards now enable individuals or groups of people to "publish" with a very low start-up cost. The computer is the modern equivalent of the eighteenth-century printer, opening its publication services to the communication needs and desires of the public. Not since the colonial printer actively encouraged members of the community to contribute essays to his newspaper has it been so easy for individuals to participate in a forum of public communication. And with the breakdown of so many other forums in which citizen interaction and communication formerly occurred—such as political parties, town meetings, and so on—this participatory function of the new press becomes all the more important.

The evolution of the First Amendment press clause in the twentieth century, however, has followed the development of American journalism. Without a press industry focused on providing opportunities and forums through which the public could easily communicate, the courts never considered such aspects to the First Amendment when articulating constitutional doctrines.

Instead of public communication, the emphasis in the courts was on the powers and freedoms of reporters and journalists. Yet now, with the possibility that an entirely new type of media industry may be emerging with the introduction of innovative communications technologies, the courts must create a First Amendment approach that can accommodate all of the various press entities.

The courts unfortunately have not reacted well to new communications technologies. With each new technology, courts have created different constitutional and regulatory models. Now with the introduction of still more communications technologies, the danger is that the courts may continue their piecemeal approach and develop a multilayered application of the First Amendment, which in turn is destined to become outdated with further technological advances.

In the coming period of change in First Amendment doctrines, the danger is that, as the government is called upon to supervise the future structuring of the media industry, the vision of the press and the First Amendment will be clouded and shaped by the old regulatory models. Although most First Amendment scholars seem to accept the need to eliminate the print-broadcast dichotomy and double standard, they nonetheless seem increasingly eager to accept the notion that the future electronic and telecommunications media will be regulated as a common carrier. They are discussing ways in which the government should regulate and oversee the future communications system. In an effort to avoid any future negative effects of a possible private monopoly, these scholars rush to permanently inject the monopoly power of government into the one area of private activity that is constitutionally insulated from the government.

It is surprising how quickly the assumption of a common carrier media has become embedded into the legal thinking about the new media. Moreover, the almost immediate conclusion that the future electronic media will be defined as common carriers presumes that the telephone companies will control this media and that, unless properly regulated, they will exert monopoly power to discriminate against other speakers or providers of information.[8] Yet what if the telephone companies do not survive the competition in the media marketplace? Even if they do, what if other competitors and new technologies arise in the future? All of these possibilities will be eliminated if government solidifies their standing with common carrier regulation. With such regulation, competition will never exist; indeed, government common carrier regulations not only cement a particular monopoly, they also inhibit any future change or progress in that medium.

In the current "media wars," the telephone companies are striving to be free of the common carrier pigeonhole. Ultimately, the telephone companies would like to provide a "video dial tone" that will allow them to transmit voice, data, and video over a national fiber-optic network. Because they want to offer such video programming and other information services, the telephone companies contend that the common carrier regulations are unfair. As one telephone executive complained, "Are we forever to be bound by reasons of history to be only common carriers, able to offer only a little programming?"[9]

The rush to impose common carrier regulations on the telecommunications media mirrors the same sentiment that favored regulation of the railroads in the nineteenth century. This fear of monopoly, however, overshadows the unique values of the First Amendment and of a free press. Information is something quite different from railroads. The expression of information, for instance, is constitutionally protected, while the transport of travelers is not. A common carrier in the eighteenth century would have been the sidewalk from which pamphlets were distributed or the post on which they were tacked. Clearly, the sidewalk or the post could not engage in the process of communication, unlike the information common carriers today.

The continuing fear of media monopolies also ignores the social trend of monopoly erosion. Industrial corporations like IBM are finding that decentralization and dispersion of corporate power is both desirable and necessary. In the long-distance telephone business, the nation's most powerful monopoly, AT&T, faces competitive pressure from Sprint and MCI, and this competition has resulted in a surge of postdivestiture vitality for AT&T. The adoption of a common carrier model of the First Amendment, however, would assure the presence of some kind of monopolized communication system. Furthermore, common carriers tend to encourage bland information and opinion that strongly contrasts with the early American press and one that may help to counteract political apathy.[10]

Common carrier regulations should not be used to deny press freedoms to an entity wishing to exercise them. Yet by categorizing the telephone companies as common carriers, for instance, the government refuses them any First Amendment freedoms and any opportunity to publish or broadcast their own information. The Constitution nowhere denies a carrier the same right as anyone else to publish without license or control. According to current regulations, however, a common carrier must have the government's permission to enter or to leave a market.[11]

The problem with viewing the First Amendment issues posed by the new media through the old common carrier regulatory lens is that such an outlook outrightly rejects any attempt to define "the press" and simply opts to perpetuate the old regulatory models in the future press. Yet common carriage should be a last resort, as suggested by Ithiel de Sola Pool.[12] Common carrier status should only be conferred on an entity *after* it has attained a clearly immovable monopoly position. Otherwise, the press will be structured by the government, which is exactly what the First Amendment's ban on licensing of the press sought to avoid. When the government designates a common carrier, it effectively and legally shuts out any competition and freezes the media into a particular status quo.

In constructing a First Amendment model for the future press, some theorists propose that the government should enact regulations that ensure diversity of opinion and high-quality programming and information. Yet these concerns are premature and inappropriate for determining press freedoms. The First Amendment does not allow the government to regulate the press in such a fine-tuned manner so as to obtain the kind of informational content that it desires. A free press cannot be regulated into existence. Government regulation cannot ensure that communication through the press be diverse, enlightened, and efficient. What if there is mandated access for many speakers, and what if they all say the same thing? What diversity will be achieved then?

In arguing for regulation of the media based on diversity of information concerns, some scholars have claimed that the telephone companies would have stronger First Amendment press rights if they provided programming or information that is substantially different from what is being provided by the existing press—newspapers and television.[13] This argument asserts that the definition of the press depends on how the particular medium treats its information and what kind of information it chooses to disseminate. If government regulations are justified on such concerns, the door has been opened to government control of information content.

Likewise, the press clause does not mandate a right of access to every member of the public who wishes to communicate through the press. The kind of access with which the press clause is concerned deals not with the access of each individual to state his or her opinion through the press, but with the kind of structural access that permits the entry of new types of press organizations and activities into society's communications system.

The demand for individual access to the media arises from the belief that, in the original print press, virtually everyone had the ability to publish his or her views in the local newspaper. This belief, however, contradicts reality. Not even the eighteenth-century press was freely accessible to every single person. The finite number of newspaper pages and the selection decisions of the printers were two significant barriers to such access. Instead, the kind of access that prevailed was the entrance of printers to the industry rather than of individuals to each newspaper, and this access resulted from the opportunities presented by a fluid and competitive industry. Entry barriers were low, and there were no governmentally protected monopolies or licensing systems. Therefore, no legal barriers and relatively few economic barriers existed to potential entrants. Those who felt strongly that their viewpoints were not being adequately presented could set up a printing press and publish their own pamphlets or newspaper. Access in First Amendment terms, therefore, meant a structural ability to change—an access bred by a freely changing press, a press industry that is open to new competitors and new communication activities.

There is nothing in First Amendment history that provides for unlimited individual access to any press entity. Even if governmental regulation structured such a press, there is no guarantee that the public would exercise such rights. In the nature of American democracy—in which the public has a limited political attention to a limited government—the people rarely speak out. Therefore, it is not important that continual access be available for any and every individual, but only that when the public chooses to forcefully speak out it has a responsive press through which to do so. The disappointing experience with public access channels on cable television, which offer continual access and which have attracted poor programming and minimal audiences, has revealed this limited tendency of the American public to speak out.[14]

The proponents of access regulation of the new media base their regulatory proposals on a "worst-case scenario" presumption of the new media. Their desire to regulate arises from the fear that the most negative kind of press will evolve from the new technologies. To encourage the full potential of the press, however, future applications of the First Amendment to the new media should incorporate an optimistic and positive view of the new press. Instead of presuming and planning for the worst scenario—such as a media that is totally monopolized and inaccessible to the public and discriminatory toward dissident ideas—the First Amendment doctrines should make room for the best of technological developments. The definition of the press should not be hinged strictly on the negative aspects of the current technologies and media entities, but should encourage the full potential of the new communication technologies and aim to fulfill the constitutional values of a free press.

Many futurists offer optimistic predictions of the new media's potential. Ithiel de Sola Pool similarly proclaimed that the new modes of communication technologies would be engines of freedom and should be regarded as "the press," free from common carrier regulations. Pool predicted that networked computers will be the printing presses of the twenty-first century, and he foresees increased competition, accessibility, and diversity in the press of the future. Likewise, Henry Geller also predicts positive developments from the new press technologies; however, to achieve this potential, he argues that governmental policy should encourage open entry, eliminate regulatory favoritism or skewing of the competition, and cease acting as a cartel manager.[15]

Despite these optimistic predictions, the changing press and the new communications technologies have caused great uncer-

tainty in the future structure and nature of the country's communications system. In the face of this uncertainty, and to better and
more rationally guide the development of society's communications system, many experts are calling for the country to develop
a communications policy. (In January 1994, the Clinton administration announced formation of a communications-and-media-
industry council that will advise the administration on information policy matters, including the implementation of a national
information infrastructure.) Experts correctly argue that America
has always shunned a national communications policy, just as it
has shunned a national economic or industrial policy. Yet the
reasons for avoiding such a national policy are not all bad. In
many ways, such a policy may conflict with the spirit and dictates
of the First Amendment, and, in another way, the First Amendment already provides the broad framework for a communications
policy. However, this framework has never been fully used because of the failure to broadly define "the press." Therefore, the
first step in forming any communications policy is to fully understand the nature and identity of "the press" as it is protected
by the First Amendment.

Once "the press" is defined, the First Amendment gives the
government permission to act only in certain ways in connection
with that press. A government policy which, for instance, promotes competition and greater participation in the press may well
be permitted under the First Amendment.[16] In stark contrast to the
past, however, the media is now calling on the government to
become a participant in the communications business by helping
to structure that business and to regulate its participants. For
instance, the development in the future of a fiber-optic network or
some other broadband telecommunications system may require
government support and assistance. But the press freedoms do not
simply belong to the established press actors—they belong to the
American public. Government intervention cannot be justified
just because some members of the press request such intervention.
Since a democratic society needs a certain type of press industry—one that is competitive, participatory, and facilitative of political dialogue—the courts must use the First Amendment to
preserve for the public the kind of social communication forum

that is necessary for the maintenance of democracy and modeled after the eighteenth-century press.

A major defect in the fourth estate model of the press was that it did not envision free press rights as belonging to the public. Instead, the fourth estate model attempted to transform the right of freedom of the press to an institutional right belonging to the established centers of recognized journalism, namely the editors and reporters of newspapers and television news departments.[17] The courts, however, have generally refused to accept such an institutional basis for freedom of the press and declined to hold that the freedom belonged only to specific institutions or organizations in society. As the Supreme Court held in *Red Lion Broadcasting Co. v. F.C.C.,* 395 U.S. 367, 390 (1969), freedom of the press is not just the right of reporters and editors, it is the people's "collective right . . . to receive suitable access to social, political, esthetic, moral and other ideas and experiences."

Though the public relies on the press as an institution of democracy, the press' freedom derives solely from the public's right to a free press through which to shape democratic society. Journalists enjoy press freedoms only because they perform constitutionally protected functions vital to a democracy.[18]

Without question, America's press will undergo great changes in the near future. And because of technological progress, the country's communications system will undoubtedly continue to change at a pace more rapid than has ever been experienced in the past. As a result of this change, the communications regulatory scheme will also face intense pressure for change. Moreover, pressures for changing the role of the press in the political process will contribute to the regulatory pressures on the media, and this changing regulatory atmosphere will inevitably translate into changes in First Amendment doctrines relating to the press.

Because constitutional freedoms are involved, it becomes vitally important to rationally guide the First Amendment into its next age. The first step in doing so involves a constitutional definition of the press which will protect the new media from restrictive and possibly suffocating regulation. In the past, new technologies have been quickly regulated without an understanding of First Amendment implications, and regulations have been adopted for technical reasons or for the protection of established interests; only in retrospect have they been seen to impair constitutional values.[19] The blinder to such First Amendment awareness has often been the confusion as to the identity of ''the press'' protected by the Constitution. The basic principle for the future is that the First Amendment should apply fully to the function of social communication, not just to the traditional media entities, and it should apply equally to both the electronic and print media.

As argued in this book, the future evolution of the media and communications environment, if it is to occur, will require supportive changes in the legal climate governing the media. Even at this book's writing new regulations have substantially affected or stunted media developments.

In February 1994, in the wake of the FCC announcement of new cable rate regulations, Bell Atlantic Corporation and Tele-Communications Inc. canceled their planned merger. Executives of the two corporations cited the new regulations as the primary reason the merger unraveled.

Southwestern Bell and Cox Enterprises Inc. also scrapped their plans to form a cable-television partnership because of increasing regulation by the FCC. After reviewing the new cable rules issued in March 1994, executives at these companies claimed that their planned partnership was no longer feasible. The new rules, as well as the fear of even more restrictive future regulations, were also being blamed for the renegotiation of several other cable–telephone company deals, including the one between Jones International Inc. and BCE Inc.

Aside from FCC regulation, antitrust rules have also shaped the recent evolution of the media. On April 5, 1994, for instance, a federal judge blocked AT&T's purchase of McCaw Cellular Communications Inc. This ruling resulted from an antitrust objection raised by BellSouth Corporation.

As these events demonstrate, the future development of the new media may be significantly hindered without a rethinking of the somewhat obsolete regulatory environment that currently exists.

NOTES
INDEX

NOTES

1. Approaching Changes in First Amendment Press Doctrines

1. On the "communications revolution," see Jeffrey Abramson, F. Christopher Arterton, and Gary R. Orren, *The Electronic Commonwealth: The Impact of the New Media Technologies on Democratic Politics* (New York: Basic Books, 1988), p. 5; on information as product, see, for example, Marc U. Porat, "Communications Policy in an Information Society," in *Communications for Tomorrow: Policy Perspectives for the 1980s,* ed. Glen O. Robinson (New York: Praeger, 1978), pp. 3–61; on earnings of producers, see Stephen Siwek, "The Export of American Culture," *The American Enterprise* (May/June 1992), 117–18.

2. This concept is raised in Todd Gitlin, *Inside Prime Time* (Pantheon, 1983).

3. Ken Auletta, *Three Blind Mice: How the TV Networks Lost Their Way* (New York: Random House, 1991).

4. Daniel Pearl, "Spurred by the Bell-TCI Deal, Congress Moves Toward Ending Cable TV-Phone Barriers," *Wall Street Journal,* 21 Oct. 1993, p. A24.

5. Christopher Lasch, "Journalism, Publicity, and the Lost Art of Argument," *Gannett Center Journal* (Spring 1990), pp. 311–48.

6. Elizabeth Kolbert, "As Political Campaigns Turn Negative," *The New York Times,* 1 May 1992, p. A11.

7. Ithiel de Sola Pool, *Technologies of Freedom: On Free Speech in an Electronic Age* (Cambridge: Belknap Press, 1983).

8. Mike Godwin, *The First Amendment in Cyberspace* (Washington, D.C.: Electronic Frontier Foundation, 1991), p. 2.

2. Historical Patterns of Change in the First Amendment

1. M. Ethan Katsh, *The Electronic Media and the Transformation of Law* (New York: Oxford University Press, 1989), p. 8; Ithiel de Sola Pool, *Technologies of Freedom: On Free Speech in an Electronic Age* (Cambridge, Belknap Press, 1983), p. 217.

2. Katsh, *The Electronic Media,* p. 16.

3. This period of First Amendment activism is discussed in Paul L. Murphy's *World War I and the Origin of Civil Liberties in the United States* (New York: Norton, 1979).

4. Michael Emery and Edwin Emery, *The Press and America: An Interpretive History of the Mass Media,* 6th ed. (Englewood Cliffs, N.J.: Prentice Hall, 1988), p. 297.

5. The appeal to a popular audience which resulted in changes in the press is discussed in John D. Stevens, *Sensationalism in the New York Press* (New York: Columbia University Press, 1991), pp. 37–45.

6. In the wake of these decisions, Zechariah Chafee published *Freedom of Speech* in 1920, a pioneering study of the First Amendment and one of the first and most important works on the First Amendment. Indeed, at the time of *Schenck,* the sparse free speech and press doctrines were unsophisticated and lacking in specificity; see Murphy, *World War I and the Origin of Civil Liberties,* pp. 39, 167; Richard Polenberg, *Fighting Faiths: The Abrams Case, the Supreme Court, and Free Speech* (New York: Viking, 1987), pp. 219, 222.

7. See Polenberg, *Fighting Faiths,* pp. 223, 227.

8. William Bulkeley, "Censorship Fights Heat Up on Academic Networks," *Wall Street Journal,* 24 May 1993, p. B1.

9. Mike Godwin, *The First Amendment in Cyberspace* (Washington, D.C.: Electronic Frontier Foundation, 1991), p. 3.

3. The Changing Press

1. Paul Farhi, "Alfred Sikes's Mission at the FCC," *The Washington Post National Weekly Edition,* 3 June 1991, p. 6.

2. Edmund Andrews, "Phone Companies Could Transmit TV Under FCC Plan," *New York Times,* 25 Oct. 1991, p. A1.

3. John Schneidawind, "Newspapers: Phone Companies' Plans a Threat," *USA Today,* 20 Feb. 1992, p. B3.

4. John Schneidawind, "The Media Go to War Over Regional Bells' Plan," *USA Today,* 18 Dec. 1991, p. B5.

5. Penny Pagano, "Electronic Warfare," *Washington Journalism Review* (Apr. 1992), p. 19.

6. Stephen Barr, "For Whom the Bells Toll," *NewsInc.* (Dec. 1991), p. 19; Schneidawind, "The Media Go to War," p. B5.

7. Barr, "For Whom the Bells Toll," p. 20; "Neuharth Breaks with Publishers," The Freedom Forum, *FLASH,* 20 Mar. 1992.

8. John Mintz, "Baby Bells, Publishers Clash on Information Services," *Washington Post,* 18 Feb. 1992, p. A1.

9. Edmund Andrews, "Cable TV Battling Phone Companies," *New York Times,* 29 Mar. 1992, p. A1; George Gilder, "Cable's Secret Weapon," *Forbes,* 13 Apr. 1992, pp. 80–84.

10. Mark Robicaux, "Cable-TV Rules Face a Blizzard of Lawsuits," *Wall Street Journal,* 9 Nov. 1992, p. B1.

11. Kirk Victor, "Broadcasters' Blues," *National Journal,* 3 Aug. 1991, p. 1925.

12. Ibid., p. 1926.

13. Ibid., p. 1927.

14. Dana Wechsler Linden and Vicki Contavespi, "Media Wars," *Forbes,* 18 Aug. 1991, p. 38

15. Victor, "Broadcasters' Blues," p. 1927.

16. Ibid., p. 1929.

17. "FCC OKs Two-Way Radio Service for TV," *Electronic Media,* 20 Jan. 1992, p. 2; Edmund Andrews, "FCC Loosens Restrictions on Owning Radio Stations," *New York Times,* 13 Mar. 1992, p. D5; Doug Halonen, "Cable Debate Tops D.C. Agenda in '92," *Electronic Media,* 20 Jan. 1992, p. 3.

18. Mary Lu Carnevale, "Cable-Phone Link Is Promising Gamble," *Wall Street Journal,* 18 May 1993, p. B1.

19. Jon Katz, "Beyond Broadcast Journalism," *Columbia Journalism Review* (Mar./Apr. 1992), pp. 19, 21.

20. Ken Auletta, "Peering Over the Edge," *Media Studies Journal* (Fall 1991), pp. 83–99.

21. Doug Underwood, "The Newspapers' Identity Crisis," *Columbia Journalism Review* (Mar./Apr. 1992), pp. 24, 26.

22. Joseph Ungaro, "Newspapers I: First the Bad News," *Media Studies Journal* (Fall 1991), pp. 101–13; Leo Bogart, "The American Media System and Its Commercial Culture," *Media Studies Journal* (Fall 1991), pp. 13–33.

23. Charles Paul Freund, "America's Past Wasteland," *The Washington Post National Weekly Edition,* 5 Aug. 1991, p. 24.

24. Pool, *Technologies of Freedom,* p. 39.

25. John Greenwald, "Wired!" *Time,* 25 Oct. 1993, p. 50.

4. The Emergence of New Media Technologies

1. Ithiel de Sola Pool, *Technologies Without Boundaries: On Telecommunications in a Global Age,* ed. Eli M. Noam (Cambridge: Harvard University Press, 1990), p. 7.

2. William Grimes, "Computer Networks Foster Cultural Chatting for Modern Times," *New York Times,* 1 Dec. 1992, p. B1; John Maxwell Hamilton, "Areopagitica Redux: In Defense of Electronic Liberties," *Media Studies Journal* (Fall 1991), p. 39

3. Julie Nicklin, "For Newly Hired Schoolteachers, an Electronic Lifeline," *Chronicle of Higher Education,* 6 Nov. 1991, p. A24.

4. Ibid., p. 40.

5. Leonard Sussman, *Power, the Press, and the Technology of Freedom: The Coming Age of ISDN* (New York: Freedom House, 1989), p. 374.

6. Frederick Williams, "Network Information Services as a New Public Medium," *Media Studies Journal* (Fall 1991), pp. 137–52.

7. Pool, *Technologies Without Boundaries,* p. 51.

8. Ibid., p. 241.

9. Philip Elmer-Dewitt, "The World on a Screen," *Time,* 21 Oct. 1991, p. 80.

10. Nicholas Negoponte, "Products and Services for Computer Networks," *Scientific American* (Sept. 1991), pp. 106–13.

11. Jeffrey Abramson, F. Christopher Arterton, and Gary R. Orren, *The Electronic Commonwealth: The Impact of the New Media Technologies on Democratic Politics* (New York: Basic Books, 1988), p. 57.

12. Ibid., p. 46.

13. Pool, *Technologies Without Boundaries,* p. 83.

14. Quotation from Pool in Gary Orren and Stephen Bates, "New Communications Technologies" (Washington, D.C.: Roosevelt Center for American Policy Studies, 1982), p. 31; on satellite transmissions, see James Traub, "Satellites: The Birds That Make It All Fly," *Channels 1984 Field Guide,* pp. 8–9.

15. Pool, *Technologies Without Boundaries,* p. 241.

16. Hamilton, "Areopagitica Redux," p. 45.

17. Ibid., p. 47. See also Abramson et al., *Electronic Commonwealth,* for a description of how candidates in the 1988 presidential election used various satellite technologies to circumvent the networks in communicating more directly with the voters (p. 103).

18. M. Ethan Katsh, *The Electronic Media, and the Transformation of Law* (New York: W. W. Norton & Co., 1979), p. 117; see also John Naisbitt, *Megatrends: Ten New Directions Transforming Our Lives*

(New York: Warner Books, 1982), pp. 159–61, and Alvin Toffler, *The Third Wave* (New York: William Morrow, 1980), pp. 416–32.

19. Katsh, *The Electronic Media,* pp. 52, 107.

20. Jordan Bonfante, "Plutocrat Populist," *Time,* 6 Apr. 1992, p. 19.

21. Abramson et al., *Electronic Commonwealth,* p. 178.

22. Pamela Varley, "Electronic Democracy," *Technology Review* (Nov. 1991), p. 44.

23. Ibid., p. 46.

24. Ibid., p. 51.

25. Abramson et al., *Electronic Commonwealth,* pp. 9, 277.

26. Ben Johnson, "Not Everyone Is Plugged In," *The Quill* (Sept. 1991), p. 32.

27. Reid Ashe, "The Human Element: Electronic Networks Succeed with Relationships, Not Information," *The Quill* (Sept. 1991), pp. 13–14.

28. John Markoff, "Staking a Claim on the Virtual Frontier," *New York Times,* 2 Jan. 1994, p. E5.

5. Political Pressures for a Changing Press

1. For a discussion of the public's confidence in the media, see Sidney M. Lipset, *The Confidence Gap: Business, Labor, and Government in the Public Mind* (New York: Free Press, 1983). According to a 22 March 1992, survey by Louis Harris and Associates, only 13 percent of those surveyed had a great deal of confidence in the press, while 87 percent had only some or hardly any confidence, or were not sure.

2. Quote from Donald Gillmor, *Power, Publicity, and the Abuse of Libel Law* (New York: Oxford University Press, 1992), p. 16; on unpopularity of press, see S. Robert Lichter and Stanley Rothman, "Media and Business Elites," *Public Opinion* (Oct./Nov. 1981), p. 15; on Grenada, see Thomas R. Dye, *Who's Running America?* (Englewood Cliffs, N.J., 1986).

3. Michael Parenti, *Democracy for the Few* (New York, 1988), p. 157; Michael Emery and Edwin Emery, *The Press and America: An Interpretive History of the Mass Media,* 6th ed. (Englewood Cliffs, N.J.: Prentice Hall, 1988), pp. 622–23, 627.

4. "How Giant TCI Uses Self-Dealing, Hardball to Dominate Market," *Wall Street Journal,* 27 Jan. 1992.

5. Ben H. Bagdikian, *The Media Monopoly,* 2nd ed. (Boston, Mass.: Beacon Press, 1987).

6. See Commission of Freedom of the Press, *A Free and Responsible Press* (Washington, D.C.: U.S. Government Printing Office, 1947), p. 80; Stephen L. Carter, "Technology, Democracy, and the Manipulation of Consent," *Yale Law Journal* 93 (1984), 603; Bruce Owen, *Economics and Freedom of Expression: Media Structure and the First Amendment* (Cambridge: Ballinger Publishing Co., 1975), pp. 26–28, 186–87; American Society of Newspaper Editors, *1990 Ownership Survey,* Apr. 1990, p. 47.

7. Leo Bogart, "The American Media System and Its Commercial Culture," *Media Studies Journal* (Fall 1991), pp. 13–33, 23, 26.

8. Nicholas Johnson and James M. Hoak, "Media Concentration," *Iowa Law Review* 56 (1970), 276; Leo Bogart, "Newspapers in Transition," *Wilson Quarterly* (Special Issue, 1982), p. 70; Philip Weiss, "Invasion of the Gannettoids," *The New Republic,* 2 Feb. 1987.

9. Quote from Gillmor, *Power, Publicity and the Abuse of Libel Law,* p. 17. Rodney Smolla, *Suing the Press: Libel, the Media, and Power* (New York: Oxford University Press, 1986), examines the recent flood of libel suits and calls it one of America's newest growth industries. He recognizes the intense sympathy of modern juries for libel plaintiffs and implies that this may be the result of the underlying public distrust of the media. Peter Stoler, *The War Against the Press: Politics, Pressure, and Intimidation in the Eighties* (New York: Dodd, Mead, 1986), also argues that large libel awards demonstrate that the ordinary citizens who make up juries feel estranged from and suspicious toward the press. A similar argument is made by Richard Clurman, *Beyond Malice: The Media's Years of Reckoning* (New Brunswick, N.J.: Transaction Books, 1988).

10. Alex Jones, "News Media's Libel Costs Rising, Study Says," *New York Times,* 26 Sept. 1991; "Juries and Damages: Comparing the Media's Libel Experience to Other Civil Litigants," *Libel Defense Resource Center Bulletin,* no. 9 (New York: LDRC, 31 Jan. 1984); Gillmor, *Power, Publicity, and the Abuse of Libel Law,* p. 19.

11. According to S. Robert Lichter, Stanley Rothman, and Linda S. Lichter, *The Media Elite: America's New Powerbrokers* (Maryland: Adler and Adler, 1986), the press today conveys a dangerously slanted left-wing bias in the presentation of the news. Edward S. Herman and Noam Chomsky, *Manufacturing Consent: The Political Economy of the Mass Media* (New York: Pantheon Books, 1988), likewise criticize the media for bias in the presentation of the news, but disagree with Lichter et al. as to the nature of that bias. According to Herman and Chomsky, the monopolized American press conveys a very narrow range of view-

points and actually slants the news with a conservative view, thereby excluding the diverse views of the majority of the people.

12. See "All the Usual Suspects: MacNeil/Lehrer and Nightline," *Extra!* (Winter 1990), special issue no. 34, pp. 7–11. In addition to a monthly newsletter, "Media Watch," and the reference book *And That's the Way It Isn't: A Reference Guide to Media Bias,* the Media Research Center also publishes *TV, etc.,* a guide to left-wing influences in the entertainment business. Challenging these groups from the left is the Fairness and Accuracy in Reporting group, founded in 1986 to oppose the media's alleged conservative bias and its corresponding unfairness toward minorities and other liberal interests. See also Joe Queenan, "The Media's Wacky Watchdogs," *Time,* 5 Aug. 1991, pp. 49–51.

13. Lichter, Rothman, and Lichter, *The Media Elite,* p. 34; Jeffrey L. Katz, "Tilt? Did the Media Favor Bill Clinton?" *Washington Journalism Review* (Jan./Feb 1993), pp. 23–28.

14. Gillmor, *Power, Publicity, and the Abuse of Libel Law,* p. 16.

15. Gillmor, *Power, Publicity, and the Abuse of Libel Law,* p. 17.

16. David Rynecki, "How Are We Doing?" *Columbia Journalism Review* (Jan. 1992), p. 15.

17. See Mitchell Hartman, "Press and Public Collide as Concern Over Privacy Rises," *The Quill* (Nov./Dec. 1990), pp. 3, 4; Louis Harris and Associates, survey Mar. 1990; Louis Harris and Associates, *The Privacy Study,* No. 902030, 1990; *Times-Mirror* study conducted by the Gallup Organization, *The People, the Press, and Politics,* 24–25 Aug. 1988 and Mar. 1986.

18. These regulations cover both per-call blocking and per-line blocking. See "An Update on Caller ID Approvals," *Privacy Journal* (Sept. 1991), p. 6; "Would FCC Preempt Stronger State Rules on Caller ID?" *Privacy Journal* (Oct. 1991), p. 1.

19. James Boylan, "Where Have All the People Gone?" *Columbia Journalism Review* (May/June 1991), pp. 33–35.

20. A critique of the media's role in the 1988 campaign is outlined in *Restoring the Bond: Connecting Campaign Coverage to Voters* (Cambridge, Mass.: Joan Shorenstein Barone Center on the Press, Politics, and Public Policy, 1991). Dan Hallin and Kiku Adatto, *Campaign Lessons for '92* (Cambridge, Mass.: Joan Shorenstein Barone Center on the Press, Politics, and Public Policy, 1991), p. 17.

21. Hallin and Adatto, *Campaign Lessons for '92,* p. 62.

22. "Citizens and Politics: A View from Main Street America," study prepared for the Kettering Foundation by the Harwood Group, June 1991; Curtis Gans, p. 17; Ruy Teixeira, *Why Americans Don't*

Vote: Turnout Decline in the United States, 1960–1984 (New York: Greenwood Press, 1987), likewise argues that the failure of many Americans to vote stems from the negative influence of the media on the conduct of politics in our society.

23. Dan Hallin and Kiku Adatto, *Campaign Lessons for '92*, 67–68; for Cronkite quote, see John Tierney, "Sound Bites Become Smaller Mouthfuls," *New York Times*, 23 Jan. 1992, p. A1.

24. Suzanne Garment, *Scandal: The Culture of Mistrust in American Politics* (New York: New York Times Books, 1991).

25. The Freedom Forum Media Studies Center, *Communiqué* (May 1992), p. 6.

26. For poll conducted by the Gallup organization, see *Newsweek*, 31 Oct. 1988, p. 19; for *Times-Mirror* poll, see Hallin and Adatto, *Campaign Lessons for '92*, p. 25.

27. For "gives people a sense," see Elizabeth Kolbert, "Political Candidates and Call-In Shows," *New York Times*, 10 June 1992, p. A20; for "lost control," see Jonathan Alter, "Why the Old Media's Losing Control," *Newsweek*, 8 June 1992, p. 28; for "galvanizing," see James Perry, "Party May Be Over for Democrats, Republicans as Candidates Use New Media," *Wall Street Journal*, 4 Nov. 1992, p. A16; for "new technologies," see Timothy Noah, "Clinton's Campaign Uses Technology to Bypass Traditional News Outlets," *Wall Street Journal*, 17 July 1992, p. A11.

28. See Patrick Garry, "Oliver Wendell Holmes and the Democratic Foundations of the First Amendment," in *Great Justices of the U.S. Supreme Court* (New York: Peter Lang, 1993).

6. The Existing Constitutional Model of the Press

1. *Nebraska Press Association v. Stuart*, 427 U.S. 539 (1976); *New York Times v. U.S.*, 403 U.S. 713 (1971).

2. Justice Potter Stewart, "Or of the Press," *Hastings Law Journal* 26 (1975), 634; *Branzburg v. Hayes* 655, 722.

3. Vincent Blasi, "The Checking Value in First Amendment Theory," *American Bar Foundation Research Journal* (1977), 523; Alexander Meiklejohn, *Free Speech and Its Relation to Self-Government* (New York: Harper & Row, 1972).

4. Benno C. Schmidt, Jr., *Freedom of the Press versus Public Access* (New York: Praeger, 1976), p. 59.

5. Timothy Gleason, *The Watchdog Concept: The Press and the*

Courts in Nineteenth-Century America (Ames: Iowa State University Press, 1990), p. 6.

6. In the companion cases of *Pell v. Procunier,* 417 U.S. 817 (1974), and *Saxbe v. Washington Post Company,* 843, the Court addressed claims by news media representatives against what they perceived as an interference with their right to gather news and upheld state and federal prison regulations which banned all personal interviews between news reporters and individually designated prison inmates. The majority of the Court in both cases treated the central issue as one of affirmative access to public information. See also Donald Gillmor, Jeromne Barron, Todd Simon, and Herbert Terry, *Mass Communication Law: Cases and Comments* (St. Paul: West Publishing Co., 1989), p. 360, for various interpretations of *Branzburg.*

7. U.S. Congress, *Newspaper Preservation Act: Hearings on H.R. 279 before the Antitrust Subcommittee of the House Committee on the Judiciary,* 91st Cong., 1st Sess., at 105, 198, 279 (1969); Bruce Owen, *Economics and Freedom of Expression: Media Structure and the First Amendment* (Cambridge: Ballinger Publishing Co., 1975), p. 49.

8. Gleason, *The Watchdog Concept,* pp. 60, 64.

9. 5 U.S.C.A., sec. 552. A sampling of cases brought under the Freedom of Information Act is presented in Gillmor and Barron, *Mass Communication Law,* pp. 457–77.

7. The Inadequacy of Existing First Amendment Models

1. Timothy Gleason, *The Watchdog Concept: The Press and the Courts in Nineteenth-Century America* (Ames: Iowa State University Press, 1990), p. viii.

2. Jerome Barron, "Access to the Press: A New First Amendment Right," *Harvard Law Review* 80 (1967), 1658; see Justice Byron White's opinions in *Branzburg v. Hayes,* 408 U.S. 665 (1972), *Zercher v. Stanford Daily,* 436 U.S. 547 (1978), *Herbert v. Lando,* 99 S.Ct. 1635 (1979), and *Gertz v. Robert Welch, Inc.,* 418 U.S. 323 (1974).

3. This is Barron's criticism of the *New York Times v. Sullivan* decision. See "Access to the Press," p. 1658.

4. John Grennwald, "Fight Now, Pay Later," *Time,* 4 Feb. 1991, p. 56.

5. See Jeffrey Abramson, F. Christopher Arterton, and Gary R. Orren, *The Electronic Commonwealth: The Impact of the New Media Technologies on Democratic Politics* (New York: Basic Books, 1988), pp. 121–22.

6. Robert W. McChesney, "An Almost Incredible Absurdity for a Democracy," *Journal of Communication Inquiry* 15, no. 1 (Winter 1991), 89–114. The Markle Commission on the Media and the Electorate, which examined the role of citizens, candidates, and the news media during the 1988 presidential election, criticized the media for the low voter turnout and the electorate's ignorance of the issues.

7. Richard Zoglin, "The Tuned-Out Generation," *Time,* 9 July 1990, p. 64.

8. Thomas Leonard, *The Power of the Press: The Birth of American Political Reporting* (New York: Oxford University Press, 1986), p. 215.

9. Larry Sabato, *Feeding Frenzy: How Attack Journalism has Transformed American Politics* (New York: Free Press, 1991); on the Pentagon official, see William Henry, "To 'Out' or Not to 'Out,'" *Time,* 19 Aug. 1991, p. 17.

10. Howard Kurtz, "Washington's Sound-Bite Superstars," *The Washington Post National Weekly Edition,* 22 July 1991, p. 6; Richard Bulliet, "Scholarship in the Public Interest: Notes from a Soundbite," *Gannett Center Journal,* p. 65.

11. According to William Greider, *Who Will Tell the People: The Betrayal of American Democracy* (New York: Simon & Schuster, 1992), pp. 7–8, journalism has become a profession with high credentials, subsidized by monopoly corporations. Consequently, news media professionals now expect generous salaries and proximity to power.

12. See Patrick Garry, *Liberalism and American Identity* (Kent, Ohio: Kent State University Press, 1992), pp. 161–85.

13. Gleason, *The Watchdog Concept,* p. 6.

8. The Historical Identity of the American Press

1. Leonard Levy, *Emergence of a Free Press* (New York: Oxford University Press, 1985), p. 272.

2. Frank L. Mott, *American Journalism: A History of Newspapers in the United States* (New York: Macmillan, 1950), p. 46; Arthur M. Schlesinger, *Prelude to Independence: The Newspaper War on Britain* (Boston: Northeastern University Press, 1980), p. 60; Donald H. Stewart, *The Opposition Press of the Federalist Period* (Albany: State University of New York Press, 1969), p. 4; William Chenery, *Freedom of the Press* (New York: Harcourt Brace, 1955), p. 144; Stewart, *Opposition Press,* p. 20.

3. Michael Emery and Edwin Emery, *The Press and America: An*

Interpretive History of the Mass Media, 6th ed. (Englewood Cliffs, N.J.: Prentice Hall, 1988), p. 68.

4. Steven Botein, "Printers and the American Revolution," in *The Press and the American Revolution,* ed. Bernard Bailyn and John Hench (Worcester: American Antiquarian Society, 1980), p. 16; Emery and Emery, *The Press and America,* p. 36.

5. Sidney Kobre, *The Development of the Colonial Newspaper* (Pittsburgh: Colonial Press, Inc., 1944), p. 147–48; Phillip Davidson, *Propaganda and the American Revolution, 1763 to 1783* (Chapel Hill, N.C.: University of North Carolina Press, 1941), p. 304.

6. Schlesinger, *Prelude to Independence,* p. 37, 165; Davidson, *Propaganda,* p. 304.

7. *Pennsylvania Gazette,* 10 June 1731.

8. "A Real Churchman," in *New York Gazeteer,* 9 Jan. 1775.

9. John Lofton, *The Press as Guardian of the First Amendment* (Charleston: University of South Carolina Press, 1980), p. 18; S. Kobre, *Foundations of American Journalism* (Westport, Conn.: Greenwood Press, 1958), p. 77. See also "The Media and the First Amendment in a Free Society," *Georgetown Law Journal* 60 (1972), 867, 879.

10. Schlesinger, *Prelude to Independence,* pp. 69, 80–82; J. T. Buckinghams, ed., *Specimens of Newspaper Literature* (Boston: C. C. Little and J. Brown, 1850), vol. 1, p. 31; Isiah Thomas, *The History of Printing in America* (New York: Weathervane Books, 1874), vol. 2, pp. 86–95; Bruce Owen, *Economics and Freedom of Expression: Media Structure and the First Amendment* (Cambridge: Ballinger Publishing Co., 1975), pp. 296–97; Schlesinger, *Prelude to Independence,* p. 143.

11. Schlesinger, *Prelude to Independence,* pp. 108–10, 119–23.

12. Robert A. Rutland, *The Newsmongers: Journalists in the Life of the Nation* (N.Y.: Dial Press, 1973), pp. 260–63.

13. Samuel Miller, qtd. in Thomas, *History of Printing,* vol. 2, p. 403.

14. Owen, *Economics and Freedom of Expression,* p. 44.

15. Ibid., p. 64.

16. John Adams, "Dissertation on the Canon and Futile Law," in *The Works of John Adams,* ed. Charles Francis Adams (Boston: Little, Brown and Co., 1851), vol. 3, p. 457; Botein, "Printers," p. 59.

17. Botein, "Printers," p. 202; G. Nash, "An Economic Interpretation of the American Revolution," *William and Mary Quarterly* 29 (1974), 199.

18. J. C. Oswald, *Printing in the Americas* (New York: Gregg Publishing Co., 1937), pp. 282–83; Schlesinger, *Prelude to Independence,* p. 58; Buel, "Freedom of the Press in Revolutionary America,"

in *The Press and the American Revolution,* ed. Bernard Bailyn and John B. Hench (Worcester: American Antiquarian Society, 1981), pp. 72–73.

19. Robert Rutland, *Birth of the Bill of Rights* (Chapel Hill, N.C.: University of North Carolina Press, 1955), p. 27; "Address to the Inhabitants of Quebec 26 October 1775," rpt. in R. Perry and J. Cooper, *Sources of Our Liberties* (Chicago: American Bar Foundation, 1952), p. 285.

20. Stewart, *Opposition Press,* pp. 4, 5, 10–11; Botein, "Printers," p. 11.

21. Mott, *American Journalism,* p. 113; Lofton, *The Press as Guardian,* p. 11.

22. J. M. Smith, *Freedom's Fetters: The Alien and Sedition Laws and American Civil Liberties* (Ithaca: Cornell University Press, 1956), p. 421; Stewart, *Opposition Press,* p. 445.

23. Smith, *Freedom's Fetters,* p. 432; Robert M. Weir, "The Role of the Newspaper Press in the Southern Colonies on the Eve of the Revolution," in Bailyn and Hench, eds., *The Press and the American Revolution,* pp. 99–100; Edmond S. Morgan, "The American Revolution Considered as an Intellectual Movement," in *Paths of American Thought,* ed. Arthur Schlesinger, Jr., and Morton White (Boston: Houghton Mifflin, 1970), pp. 11–33.

24. Thomas Leonard, *The Power of the Press: The Birth of American Political Reporting* (New York: Oxford University Press, 1986).

9. The Independent Nature of the First Amendment Press Clause

1. Justice Potter Stewart, "Or of the Press," *Hastings Law Journal* 26 (1975), 631.

2. *Cohen v. California,* 403 U.S. 15 (1971); *U.S. v. O'Brien,* 391 U.S. 367 (1968); *Brandenburg v. Ohio,* 395 U.S. 444 (1969); *Communist Party v. Subversive Activities Control Board,* 367 U.S. 1 (1961); *U.S. v. Robel,* 389 U.S. 258 (1967); *Gregory v. City of Chicago,* 394 U.S. 111 (1967); *Lloyd Corp. v. Tanner,* 407 U.S. 551 (1972); *Miller v. California,* 413 U.S. 15 (1973).

3. *Texas v. Johnson,* 109 S.Ct. 2533 (1990).

4. Stewart, "Or of the Press," p. 631.

5. R. Jebb, ed., *Commentary of John Milton* (Cambridge: Oxford University Press, 1918); John Stuart Mill, *On Liberty,* p. 18.

6. Archibald Cox, *Freedom of Expression* (Cambridge: Harvard University Press, 1981), p. 2; Jeffrey Smith, *Printers and Press Free-*

dom: The Ideology of Early American Journalism, p. 32; *Journals of the Continental Congress* 1 (1776), 104, qtd. in *Near v. Minnesota,* 283 U.S. 697 (1931).

7. Zechariah Chafee, *Free Speech in the United States* (Cambridge: Harvard University Press, 1942), p. 31; Alexander Meiklejohn, *Free Speech and Its Relation to Self-Government* (New York: Harper & Row, 1972), pp. 26–27.

8. The most famous statement of Holmes's "marketplace of ideas" concept appears in his dissent in *Abrams v. United States,* 250 U.S. 616, 630 (1919).

9. This view was also restated in *Red Lyon Broadcasting Company v. FCC,* 395 U.S. 367, 390 (1969.

10. On the amendment's primary purpose, see *Mills v. Alabama,* 384 U.S. 214, 218 (1966); On the political role of the press, see David Anderson, "Origins of the Press Clause," *UCLA Law Review* 30 (1983), 490; for Madison's quote, see James Boylan, "Where Have All the People Gone?" *Columbia Journalism Review* (May/June 1991), p. 34.

11. *Herbert v. Lando,* 441 U.S. 153, 184 (Powers, J., concurring). On free expression, see *Buckley v. Valeo,* 424 U.S. 1, 14 (1976); *City of Chicago v. Mosley,* 408 U.S. 92, 95 (1972); *Red Lyon Broadcasting Company v. FCC,* 395 U.S. 367, 390 (1969).

12. Alexander Meiklejohn, *Political Freedom: The Constitutional Powers of the People* (New York: Harper & Row, 1960), p. 75; see also Meiklejohn, *Free Speech,* pp. 26–27, 88–89; Meiklejohn, "The First Amendment Is an Absolute," *Supreme Court Review* (1961), p. 245.

13. Melvin B. Nimmer, "Is Freedom of the Press a Redundancy," *Hastings Law Journal* 26 (1975), 653.

14. John Hart Ely, *Democracy and Distrust* (Cambridge: Harvard University Press, 1980), p. 112.

15. See the following for John Hart Ely's process-view of the Constitution: Ely, *Democracy and Distrust;* Ely, "The Supreme Court, 1977 Term," *Harvard Law Review* 92 (1978), 5; Ely, "Toward a Representation Reinforcing Mode of Judicial Review," *Maryland Law Review* 37 (1978), 451.

16. Thomas Emerson, *The System of Freedom of Expression* (New York: Random House, 1970), pp. 6–7. See also Thomas Leonard, *The Power of the Press: The Birth of American Political Reporting* (New York: Oxford University Press, 1986), p. 6. Leonard argues that the constitutional creation of a republican style of government did not necessarily create democratic participation in that government. This latter achievement was left to the press. Through political dialogue in the press, the public learned how to participate in the democratic process.

17. Ithiel de Sola Pool, *Technologies of Freedom: On Free Speech in an Electronic Age* (Cambridge, Belknap Press, 1983), pp. 9–10, 234–40, 246.

18. David Schuman, "Our Fixation on Rights Is Dysfunctional and Deranged," *Chronicle of Higher Education,* Apr. 1, 1992, p. B1.

19. Julius Stone, *The Province and Function of Law* (Cambridge: Harvard University Press, 1950), pp. 520–21; Hannah Arendt, *The Human Condition* (Chicago: University of Chicago Press, 1958), p. 176; Karl Deutsch, *Nationalism and Social Communication: An Inquiry Into the Foundations of Nationality,* 2nd ed. (Cambridge: Wiley, 1966).

20. Arendt, *The Human Condition,* p. 8.

21. Jeffrey B. Abramson, F. Christopher Arterton, and Gary R. Orren, *The Electronic Commonwealth: The Impact of the New Media Technologies on Democratic Politics* (New York: Basic Books, 1988), p. 22; John Dewey, *Freedom and Culture* (New York: Paragon Books, 1939), p. 6; Franklyn S. Haiman, *Speech and Law in a Free Society* (Chicago: University of Chicago Press, 1981), p. 3.

22. Leonard Levy, *Emergence of a Free Press* (New York: Oxford University Press, 1985), in studying early America and the remarkable freedom enjoyed by the colonial press, similarly found that colonial Americans regarded a free press as a necessity to a democratic government (p. x). In *The Electronic Commonwealth,* the authors describe their ideal of a communitarian democracy and how the new press may support that ideal. A communitarian democracy is essentially a participatory democracy, in which all citizens have the opportunity and are encouraged to participate directly in government. For the communitarian,

> No extension of voting on secret ballots can overcome the alienation between citizen and citizen or sponsor the public debate that alone makes participation in government a course in civic education . . . what is required is participation in the deliberations and persuasions that distinguish the democratic process. (P. 23)

Consequently, not only is there a connection between community and democracy, but only a participatory press can build a participatory democracy.

23. Haiman, *Speech and Law,* p. 6; Emerson, *The System of Freedom of Expression,* pp. 6–7.

24. Jerome Barron, "Access to the Press: A New First Amendment Right," *Harvard Law Review* 80 (1967), 1650.

25. David Richards, "Free Speech and Obscenity Law: Toward a Moral Theory of the First Amendment," *University of Pennsylvania*

Law Review 123 (1974), has said that the value of free expression "rests on its deep relation to self-respect arising from autonomous self-determination without which the life of the spirit is meager and slavish" (45).

26. C. Edwin Baker, "Press Rights and Government Power to Structure the Press," *University of Miami Law Review* 34 (1980), remarks that since the press is a commercial enterprise, it lacks the individual liberty and self-realization aspects of speech that justify its constitutional protection for individuals. Thus, the value of individual liberty is not closely connected with the activities of the press (819).

27. Chafee, *Free Speech in the United States,* pp. 31–35.

28. *Richmond Newspapers, Inc., v. Virginia,* 448 U.S. 555, 588 (1980) (Brennan, J., concurring); Donald Gillmor, Jeromne Barron, Todd Simon, and Herbert Terry, *Mass Communication Law: Cases and Comments* (St. Paul: West Publishing Co., 1989), pp. 8–9.

29. Extract from *Saxbe v. Washington Post Co.,* 417 U.S. 817, 862; see also Lillian R. BeVier, "Justice Powell and the First Amendment's Societal Function," *Virginia Law Review* 68 (1982), 177. See also Melvin B. Nimmer, *Freedom of Speech* (New York: Matthew Bender and Co., 1984), p. 4.

30. Baker, "Press Rights," p. 859.

31. James Carey, Daniel Hallin, and other media scholars have noted the connection between the press and public life. They argue that newspapers came into existence as an important auxiliary to political debate almost with the emergence of legislative and electoral politics. See Boylan, "Where Have All the People Gone?," p. 34.

32. Randall Bezanson, "The New Free Press Guarantee," *Virginia Law Review* 63 (1977), 732; Baker, "Press Rights," pp. 825, 827.

33. Stewart, "Or of the Press," pp. 631, 633.

34. Pool, *Technologies of Freedom,* pp. 9–10.

35. Thomas Jefferson, *The Papers of Thomas Jefferson,* ed. J. Boyd (Princeton: Princeton University Press, 1950), vol. I, p. 363.

36. Arthur M. Schlesinger, *Prelude to Independence* (New York: Alfred A. Knopf, 1958), pp. 163–86.

10. The Press, Politics, and the Democratic Dialogue

1. The views of John Dewey are discussed in Robert B. Westbrook, *John Dewey and American Democracy* (Ithaca, N.Y.: Cornell University Press, 1991). See also Jeffrey B. Abramson, F. Christopher Arterton, and Gary R. Orren, *The Electronic Commonwealth: The Impact of New*

Media Technologies on Democratic Politics (New York: Basic Books, 1988), p. 241.

2. In a notable series of books, *Public Opinion* (New York: Harcourt Brace and Co., 1922), and *The Phantom Public* (New York: Harcourt Brace, 1925), Walter Lippmann argued that popular participation in public affairs should be circumscribed because of citizens' limited knowledge and their tendency toward hedonistic distraction.

3. Dan Hallin, *Columbia Journalism Review* (Jan./Feb. 1991).

4. Robert Bellah, Richard Madsen, William Sullivan, Ann Swidler, and Steven Tipton, *Habits of the Heart: Individualism and Commitment in American Life* (Berkeley and Los Angeles: University of California Press, 1985).

5. Michael Deaver, "Perot Stresses Hominess," *New York Times,* May 26, 1992, p. A1, illustrates this point in describing Ross Perot's strategy to strengthen his presidential image: "It was a very smart move to pick up on the talk show concept. I think Perot understands something fundamental about what is going on in this country with talk radio and TV programs. They have become the track the disenfranchised now uses to express its will. The elite press is part of the establishment, as far as the public is concerned, part of the whole rigged game, part of the fix."

6. "Citizens and Politics: A View from Main Street America," study prepared for the Kettering Foundation by the Harwood Group, June 1991.

7. Abramson et al., *The Electronic Commonwealth,* pp. 14, 23.

8. Robert N. Bellah, Richard Madsen, William M. Sullivan, Ann Swidler, and Steven M. Tipton, *The Good Society* (New York: Alfred A. Knopf, 1989).

9. W. Phillips Davison, "Mass Media, Civic Organizations, and Street Gossip: How Communication Affects the Quality of Life in an Urban Neighborhood," Gannett Center for Media Studies working paper, 1988, p. 24.

10. Daniel Yankelovich, *Coming to Public Judgment: Making Democracy Work in a Complex World* (Syracuse, N.Y.: Syracuse University Press, 1991).

11. James Fishkin, *Democracy and Deliberation: New Directions for Democratic Reform* (New Havenn: Yale University Press, 1991); James Carey, qtd. in James Boylan, "Where Have All the People Gone?" *Columbia Journalism Review,* May/June 1991, p. 35.

12. The need for such dialogue has been recognized in a feasibility study by Alvin H. Perlmutter, Inc., for the John and Mary Markle Foundation. This study proposed the creation of a company, "The Voters'

Channel," to stimulate new political programming which would present voters' concerns and provide candidates with air time for direct communication. Robert Entman, *Democracy Without Citizens,* qtd. in Boylan, "Where Have All The People Gone?," p. 34, proposes the restoration of the politically underwritten press of the early nineteenth century "to foster the dissemination of more diversity, more readily accessible ideas."

13. Mary Ann Glendon, *Rights Talk: The Impoverishment of Political Discourse* (New York: Free Press, 1991); M. L. Stein, "Newspapers as Wimps," *Editor & Publisher,* Feb. 22, 1992, pp. 10, 35.

14. Jay Rosen, "The Erosion of Public Time," *The Quill* (Sept. 1991), pp. 22–23.

15. Christopher Lasch, "Journalism, Publicity, and the Lost Art of Argument," *Gannett Center Journal* (Spring 1990).

16. Abramson et al., *The Electronic Commonwealth,* p. 74.

17. Quotes from Michael Emery and Edwin Emery, *The Press and America: An Interpretive History of the Mass Media,* 6th ed. (Englewood Cliffs, N.J.: Prentice Hall, 1988), p. 118. See also Abramson et al., *The Electronic Commonwealth,* pp. 80–81.

18. Lawrence Goodwyn, *Democratic Promise: The Populist Moment in America* (New York: Oxford University Press, 1981); for statistics, see Emery and Emery, *The Press and America,* p. 188.

19. Emery and Emery, *The Press and America,* pp. 194, 255.

20. Goodwyn, *Democratic Promise,* p. 206.

21. Arlow Andersen, *Rough Road to Glory: The Norwegian-American Press Speaks Out on Public Affairs, 1875–1925;* Alan Metcalf, "Jewish Newspapers in America," *Media History Digest,* pp. 22–29. The most influential and widely read Yiddish newspaper, *The Forward,* was founded in 1897 and "functioned less as journalism than as dialogue within the immigrant community" (p. 23). It even performed such "community bulletin board" services as publishing letters from abandoned wives left in the Old World by immigrant husbands. Like the immigrant press in general, the Jewish press frequently took on controversial political subjects and helped their readers take political action on matters of concern to new immigrants.

22. Goodwyn, *Democratic Promise,* p. 288.

23. By 1970 there were 1,700 religious magazines, including 1,100 Protestant, 400 Catholic, and 200 Jewish. See Emery and Emery, *The Press and America,* p. 444.

24. Ibid., pp. 481, 482. See also Abe Peck, *Uncovering the Sixties: The Life and Times of the Underground Press* (New York: Pantheon, 1985), pp. 31–40.

25. Jean Ward and Cecilie Gaziano, "A New Variety of Urban Press: Neighborhood Public-Affairs Publications," *Journalism Quarterly* 53 (Spring 1976), 61–67.

11. Unifying the First Amendment for a Converging Press

1. David Bollier, "Electronic Media, Regulation, and the First Amendment: A Perspective for the Future," *Forum Report* (conference of the Aspen Institute's program on communications and society), 1991, p. 11.

2. Lena Williams, "The Party Winds Down on Socializing by Phone," *New York Times,* Aug. 31, 1988.

3. M. Ethan Katsh, *The Electronic Media, and the Transformation of Law* (New York: Oxford University Press, 1989), pp. 164–66. For quote, see David Lange, "The Speech and Press Clauses," *UCLA Law Review* 23 (1975), 77, 106.

4. Monroe Price, "Redefining the First Amendment: The Role of the New Technology," in *Electronic Publishing Plus: Media for a Technological Future,* ed. Martin Greenberger (G. K. Hall, 1985), p. 264.

5. In *Metromedia v. City of San Diego,* 453 U.S. 490, 501 (1961), the Court stated that "Different characteristics of different media have created for each method of communicating . . . a law unto itself, reflecting the differing natures, values, abuses and dangers of each method."

6. The computer, incidentally, suffered the same misperception a century later. See Ithiel de Sola Pool, *Technologies of Freedom: On Free Speech in an Electronic Age* (Cambridge, Belknap Press, 1983), pp. 98, 91. Pool, a noted communications law scholar, illustrates the surprising but glaring absence of any reference to the First Amendment in the early court decisions involving the regulation of the telegraph and telephone (p. 81).

7. Don R. Pember, *Mass Media Law* 4th ed. (Carmel, Ind.: Brown & Benchmark, 1987), p. 550.

8. Pool, *Technologies of Freedom,* p. 137.

9. Ibid., p. 161.

10. *National Association of Broadcasters v. F.C.C.,* 740 F.2d 1190, 1202 (C.C. Cir. 1984), quoting the legislative history of the Radio Act of 1927, 67 Cong. Rec. 5557, 5558 (1926). Donal E. Lively, "Fear and the Media: A First Amendment Horror Show," *Minnesota Law Review* 69, no. 5 (May 1985), 1071.

11. Pool, *Technologies of Freedom,* p. 39; quote from A. L. Eisen-

berg, *Children and Radio Programs* (New York: Columbia University Press, 1936), p. 91.

12. *Mutual Film Corp. v. Industrial Comm'n,* 236 U.S. 230, 244 (1915), overruled by *Joseph Burstyn, Inc. v. Wilson,* 343 U.S. 495, 501 (1952). As the Court later acknowledged, "It cannot be doubted that motion pictures are a significant medium for the communication of ideas."

13. Quote from Lively, "Fear and the Media," p. 1078. Courts have expressed concern with "the subliminal impact of this pervasive propaganda, which may be heard even if not listened to, and may reasonably be thought greater than the impact of the written word." *Banzhaf v. F.C.C.,* 405 F.2d 1082, 1100 (D.C. Cir. 1968).

14. Ithiel de Sola Pool, *Forecasting the Telephone: A Retrospective Technology Assessment of the Telephone* (Norwood, N.J.: Ablex, 1983), p. 125.

15. Pool, *Technologies of Freedom,* p. 50; for quote, see *First Amendment: The Challenge of New Technology,* ed. Sig Mickelson with Elena Mier Y Teran (San Diego: San Diego Communications Council, 1987), p. 41.

16. Philip Elmer-Dewitt, "Cyberpunks and the Constitution," *Time,* Apr. 8, 1991, p. 81.

17. The assumption underlying such constitutional relativity is that "each [medium] tends to present its own peculiar problems." See *Joseph Burstyn, Inc. v. Wilson,* 343 U.S. 495, 503 (1952).

18. Pool, *Technologies of Freedom,* pp. 157, 171.

19. Henry Geller and Donna Lampert, "Constitutional and Policy Issues with the New Informational Services: The Structural Versus Behavioral Approach," in *Electronic Publishing Plus,* p. 273.

20. Quote from Lively, "Fear and the Media," p. 1092; see Koppel, "Applicability of Equal Time Doctrine," *Harvard Journal of Legislation* 20, 536–37, for criticism on the new media's cumulative impact.

21. "Burdensome regulation": Edmund L. Andrews, "Rerun Rights Proposal Angers Hollywood Studios," *New York Times,* 7 Apr. 1991; on negotiation process, see *Evaluation of the Syndication and Financial Interest Rules,* 6 F.C.C. Rec. 3094 (1991). See also *Fox Broadcasting Company Request for Temporary Waiver of Certain Provisions of 47 C.F.R. Sec. 73.658,* 5 F.C.C. Rec. 3211 (1990).

22. But, as Boylan, "Where Have All The People Gone?," p. 35, argues, "journalism remains the one non-official institution that is not, or at least should not be, itself a special interest. As such, it may in the long run be able to occupy a critical role in re-establishing a sense of

common interests and common welfare. It can begin by seeking to emphasize its role of widening and deepening public discussion.''

23. See Joseph Friedberg, "Industry Stocks Take a Beating," *Electronic Media,* 27 May 1991, p. 3; *Cable World,* 22 Apr. 1991, p. 3; *Cable World,* Nov. 19, 26, 1991; Multichannel News, 22 Apr. 1991, p. 42. See particularly Doug Halonen, "Sikes: TV Future Belongs to Cable," *Electronic Media,* 18 May 1992. On slowing development of cable, see former FCC Commissioner Anne Jones, speech Feb. 14, 1983 to Univ. of Cincinnati School of Law: "During much of the time the FCC was impeding development of . . . cable in order to protect conventional television." Even more bluntly, Commissioner Jones, at a Washington, D.C., speech on 29 Oct. 1982, stated: "Commission deliberately regulated this technology [cable] in such a way as to hinder its development."

24. Harold Farrow and Sol Schildhause, "The Telecommunications Mosiac," *Communications Law* 1 (1991), 401–22, 405; *Broadcasting Magazine,* 13 Aug. 1990, p. 27; Robert Bruce, "FCC Watch," *Cable TV and New Media* 9, no. 10 (Dec. 1991), p. 2. The FCC has also proposed a dramatic expansion of television ownership limits from twelve to twenty-four stations. Doug Halonen, "FCC Seeks to Open TV Ownership," *Electronic Media,* May 18, 1992, p. 1.

25. Jonathan W. Emord, *Freedom, Technology, and the First Amendment* (San Francisco: Pacific Research Institute for Public Policy, 1991), p. 124.

26. Lively, "Fear and the Media," p. 1094.

27. Pool, *Technologies of Freedom,* p. 23.

28. Jeffrey Abramson, F. Christopher Arterton, and Gary R. Orren, *The Electronic Commonwealth: The Impact of the New Media Technologies on Democratic Politics* (New York: Basic Books, 1988), p. 259.

29. On "fatal flaws" in broadcast regulation, see, e.g., Ronald H. Coase, "The Federal Communications Commission," *Journal of Law and Economics* 2 (1959), 1; Emord, *Freedom, Technology, and the First Amendment,* p. 29; see also Pool, *Technologies of Freedom,* p. 51. Bruce Owen, "The Role of Print in an Electronic Society," in *Communications for Tomorrow: Policy Perspectives for the 1980s,* ed. Glen O. Robinson (New York: Praeger, 1978), argues that media regulation has had a definite censorship affect on message content (p. 34). Studies on the telecommunications industry as an unnatural monopoly are cited in John T. Wenders, "Unnatural Monopoly in Telecommunications," *Telecommunications Policy* (Jan./Feb. 1992), p. 13. On DuMont, see Jon Krampner, "Case of the Fourth Network," *Media History Digest* (Fall 1990), pp. 32–40.

30. Seigenthaler quote from Bill Monroe, "The Slow Poisoning of the First Amendment," *1991 First Amendment Law Handbook,* ed. James Swanson (New York: Clark, Boardman Callaghan, 1991), pp. 29–39, 37. On Hendricks, see Bill Carter, "Now or in 1993, Cable TV Meets the Regulators," *New York Times,* 8 Mar. 1992, p. A1.

31. Mickelson, *The First Amendment,* p. 41.

32. Price, "Redefining the First Amendment," p. 258.

33. Abramson et al., *Electronic Commonwealth,* p. 252.

34. See Pool, *Technologies of Freedom,* p, 244; Bollier, "Electronic Media, Regulation, and the First Amendment," p. 2. The scarcity rationale is set forth in *Red Lion Broadcasting Company v. F.C.C.,* 395 U.S. 367 (1969). Quote by Tauzin from Daniel Pearl, "Spurred by the Bell-TCI Deal, Congress Moves Toward Ending Cable TV–Phone Barriers," *Wall Street Journal,* 21 Oct. 1993, p. A24.

35. Emord, *Freedom, Technology, and the First Amendment,* p. 111.

36. *Report,* MM Docket No. 89–600, 13 July 1990.

37. *Comments of Competitive Cable Association,* Attachment 1, p. 4, in FCC's Docket MM 90–4 (effective competition proceeding).

38. Lively, "Fear and the Media," pp. 1093, 1097.

12. Applying the First Amendment to the New Press

1. Bruce Owen, *Economics and Freedom of Expression: Media Structure and the First Amendment* (Cambridge: Ballinger Publishing Co., 1975), pp. 43–44; on passive citizenry, see David Bollier, "Electronic Media, Regulation, and the First Amendment: A Perspective for the Future," *Forum Report* (conference of the Aspen Institute's program on communications and society), 1991, p. 12.

2. Justice Blackmun's dissent criticized this interest-group approach and favored the approach taken by the Minnesota Supreme Court. That court's decision, according to Blackmun, was "premised not on the identity of the speaker, but on the speech itself" (111 S.Ct. at 2520).

3. As argued by Justice Souter in his dissent, "the First Amendment goes beyond protection of the press and the self-expression of individuals to prohibit government from limiting the stock of information from which members of the public may draw" (111 S.Ct. at 2523).

4. The problems and development of interest-group politics is discussed in Theodore J. Lowi, *The End of Liberalism: Ideology, Policy, and the Crisis of Public Authority* (New York: W. W. Norton & Co.,

1969), and in Alonzo Hamby, *Liberalism and Its Challengers: FDR to Reagan* (New York: Oxford University Press, 1985).

5. Lawrence K. Grossman, "Regulate the Medium, Liberate the Message: Original Intent in the Electronic Age," *Columbia Journalism Review* (Nov. 1991), p. 74.

6. Geller qtd. in Bollier, *Electronic Media, Regulation, and the First Amendment,* p. 12. Ithiel de Sola Pool advocates a similar approach in *Technologies of Freedom: On Free Speech in an Electronic Age* (Cambridge: Belknap Press, 1983), see esp. p. 16.

7. Leonard Sussman, *Power, the Press and the Technology of Freedom: The Coming Age of ISDN* (New York: Freedom House, 1989), p. 424.

8. These fears and presumptions are illustrated in Bollier, *Electronic Media, Regulation, and the First Amendment,* pp. 00–00.

9. Ibid., p. 10.

10. For a discussion of deregulation trends, see Richard Wiley, "The Media and the Communications Revolution: An Overview of the Regulatory Framework and Developing Trends," *Communications Law* 3 (1991), 12–33, 14.

11. See *U.S. v. American Tel. & Tel. Co.,* 552 F. Supp. 131 (D.D.C. 1982), aff'd sub nom. *Maryland v. U.S.,* 103 S.Ct. 1240 (1983).

12. Pool, *Technologies of Freedom,* pp. 31–32.

13. Daniel L. Brenner, "Divergent Regulation of New Communications Technologies," in *Visions of the First Amendment for a New Millennium,* ed. Fred Cate (Washington, D.C.: The Annenberg Washington Program, 1992), pp. 47–58, 53.

14. Daniel L. Brenner, "Cable Television and the Freedom of Expression," in *1991 First Amendment Law Handbook,* ed. James Swanson (New York: Clark, Boardman Callaghan, 1991), pp. 287–319, 294.

15. "Spectacular advances in communication technology," according to Alvin Toffler, "open, for the first time, a mind-boggling array of possibilities for direct citizen participation in political decision-making." See Alvin Toffler, *The Third Wave* (New York: William Morrow, 1980), p. 429. This theme is echoed by John Naisbitt, *Megatrends: Ten New Directions Transforming Our Lives* (New York: Warner Books, 1982), p. 160; Pool, *Technologies of Freedom,* p. 117; Henry Geller, "Regulation and Government Policy," *Media Studies Journal* (Nov. 1991), pp. 171–72.

16. Since the press clause confers a positive liberty, it can tolerate government action that supports the press functions protected by the First Amendment. Historically, government intervention has been used to encourage the full exercise of press freedom. Examples include postal

subsidies, statutes protecting the identity of news sources, and the antitrust exemption for once-competing newspapers' joint operating agreements. Indeed, postal deficits have historically accompanied the growth of the press. From the 1790s until 1918, with the exception of a temporary increase during the War of 1812, Congress never approved any increase in postage rates for newspapers. See Pool, *Technologies of Freedom,* p. 79.

17. This argument is made by Timothy Gleason, *The Watchdog Concept: The Press and the Courts in Nineteenth-Century America* (Ames: Iowa State University Press, 1990), pp. 99, 103, 109.

18. See, for example, Alexander Meiklejohn, *Free Speech and Its Relation to Self-Government* (New York: Harper and Brothers, 1948), pp. 26–27, 93–94.

19. Pool, *Technologies of Freedom,* p. 189.

INDEX OF CASES

Pitt Series in Policy and Institutional Studies

Bert A. Rockman, Editor

The Presidency and Public Policy Making
George C. Edwards III, Steven A. Shull, and Norman C. Thomas, Editors

Pressure, Power, and Policy: Policy Networks and State Autonomy in Britain and the United States
Martin J. Smith

Private Markets and Public Intervention: A Primer for Policy Designers
Harvey Averch

The Promise and Paradox of Civil Service Reform
Patricia W. Ingraham and David H. Rosenbloom, Editors

Public Policy in Latin America: A Comparative Survey
John W. Sloan

Reluctant Partners: Implementing Federal Policy
Robert P. Stoker

Researching the Presidency: Vital Questions, New Approaches
George C. Edwards III, John H. Kessel, and Bert A. Rockman, Editors

Roads to Reason: Transportation, Administration, and Rationality in Colombia
Richard E. Hartwig

Scrambling for Protection: The New Media and the First Amendment
Patrick Garry

The SEC and Capital Market Regulation: The Politics of Expertise
Ann M. Khademian

Site Unseen: The Politics of Siting a Nuclear Waste Repository
Gerald Jacob

The Speaker and the Budget: Leadership in the Post-Reform House of Representatives
Daniel J. Palazzolo

The State Roots of National Politics: Congress and the Tax Agenda, 1978–1986
Michael B. Berkman

The Struggle for Social Security, 1900–1935
Roy Lubove

Tage Erlander: Serving the Welfare State, 1946–1969
Olof Ruin

Thatcher, Reagan, Mulroney: In Search of a New Bureaucracy
Donald Savoie

Traffic Safety Reform in the United States and Great Britain
Jerome S. Legge, Jr.

Urban Alternatives: Public and Private Markets in the Provision of Local Services
Robert M. Stein

The U.S. Experiment in Social Medicine: The Community Health Center Program, 1965–1986
Alice Sardell